PRINT'S BEST LETTERHEADS & BUSINESS CARDS

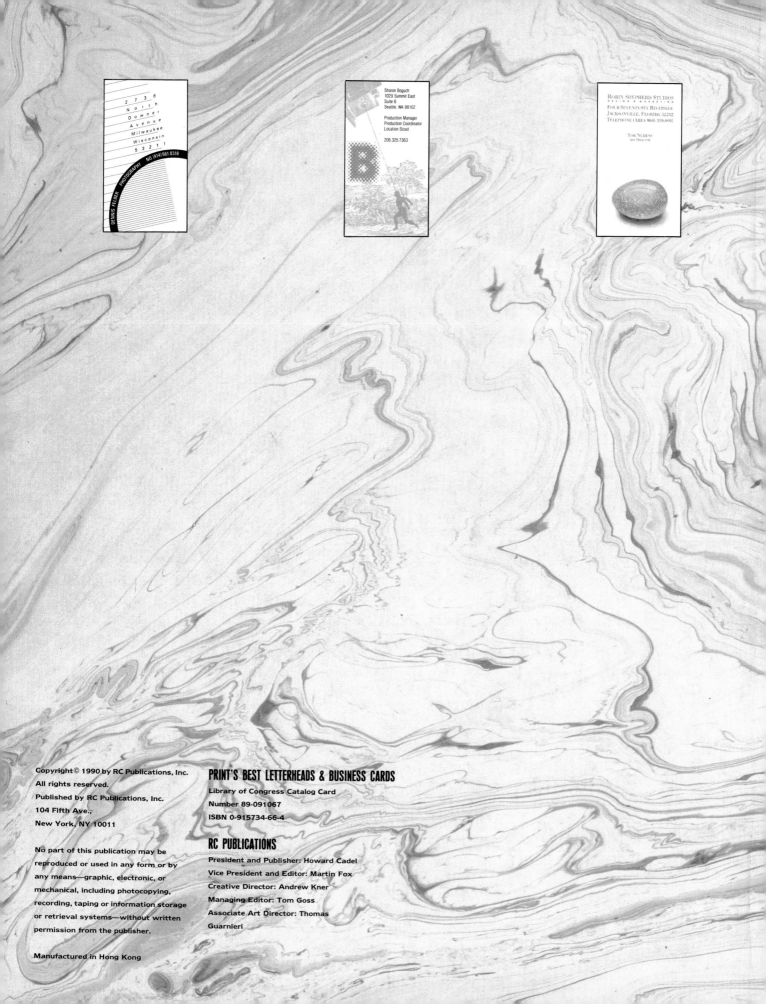

PRINT'S BEST LETTERHEADS & BUSINESS CARDS

Library of Congress Catalog Card
Number 89-091067
ISBN 0-915734-66-4

RC PUBLICATIONS

President and Publisher: Howard Cadel
Vice President and Editor: Martin Fox
Creative Director: Andrew Kner
Managing Editor: Tom Goss
Associate Art Director: Thomas
Guarnieri

Print's Best
LETTERHEADS &
BUSINESS CARDS
WINNING DESIGNS FROM PRINT MAGAZINE'S NATIONAL COMPETITION

Edited by
TOM GOSS

Art Directed by
ANDREW KNER

Designed by
THOMAS GUARNIERI

Published by
RC PUBLICATIONS, INC.
NEW YORK, NY

INTRODUCTION

Letterheads, business cards and other items of stationery are the most basic components of any graphic identity system. Indeed, before most start-up businesses even have a product to sell, they commission a designer to create a logo and, at the very least, a business card. It is because stationery systems do occupy such an essential position in communications that the editors of PRINT felt that a book on letterheads and business cards would be a logical companion volume to our simultaneously published *Print's Best Logos & Symbols.*

The extent to which stationery systems are quite consciously used, not only to identify, but to project the personality of the sender may be illustrated by the common practice among corporations and other institutions of using two letterhead designs: one considered "formal," for occasions of importance, and another, more workaday, letterhead for routine correspondence and business. Most often, the informal letterhead is a simplified version of a more elaborate formal version, and this practice is probably the most common manifestation of a trend in stationery design known as "kinetic identity."

The central idea of kinetic identity is that each piece of a stationery system represents another opportunity to communicate the image the sender wants to project to the recipient. Each piece is not, therefore, stamped with the same symbol or logo treatment, but shares characteristics with the other parts of the system while containing differences that enhance the message of the whole system. In a stationery system for a general contractor reproduced in this volume, for example, the logo consists of the firm's name and address accompanied by a line drawing of a different hand tool for each piece in the system. The type and drawing styles are consistent on each piece, and the overall impression is one of professionalism and versatility—very desirable qualities in a general contractor.

CONTENTS

INTRODUCTION . . . . PAGES 4,5

STATIONERY SYSTEMS . . . . . PAGES 6-173

INDEX . . . . PAGES 174-176

Not surprisingly, the letterheads and business cards that designers create for themselves best demonstrate the ability of stationery to project personality. In their enthusiasm for creating something to please themselves, designers have devised stationery systems that are among the most original, resourceful and witty of all the examples presented in this volume. But designers are not the only professional group notable for their superior letterheads. As the staff of PRINT has noticed for years, stationery programs for dentists have been especially appealing—more so than for almost any other group of professionals. This has been attributed to the nearly universal dread of visits to the dentist's office and dentists' attempts to depict themselves as sensitive, approachable healthcare professionals.

Other categories of clients included in this collection are illustrators, architects and photographers, as well as corporations, hotels, restaurants, and writers. All told, there are 129 different "programs" reproduced here, although it should be noted that some of these consist of just a single piece—business cards in most cases—either because the single piece was all that was available from a system no longer in use, or because it was all the client could afford. All these programs, whatever they consist of, were previously published in PRINT's Regional Design Annual, which is itself the product of a national design competition judged by the editors and art director of PRINT. The business cards, letterheads and other items of stationery are shown much larger and more extensively than they appeared in the Annual. No effort has been made to force the wide variety of work into arbitrary categories. Instead, the stationery programs are presented in a sequence designed to be visually stimulating and to provide creative insight. It is our belief that this approach not only shows the fine work collected here in the best possible light, but enhances this book's usefulness as a reference tool as well. —*Tom Goss*

1901 CAPITOL AVENUE
SACRAMENTO, CA 95814
PHONE 916 448 1901

MONIGHAN TERRY
ARCHITECTS AIA

DESIGN FIRM: The
Dunlavey Studio,
Sacramento, California
ART DIRECTOR: Michael
Dunlavey
DESIGNER: Kevin Yee

Monighan + Terry Architects, A.I.A.

TAMARA LILLER
PHOTOGRAPHY

700 7th STREET, S.W. #418
WASHINGTON, D.C. 20024-2446
(202) 488-3710

DESIGNER/ILLUSTRATOR:

Margaret Georgiann,

Annandale, Virginia

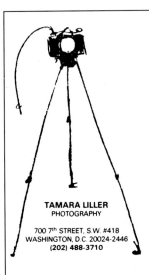

DESIGN FIRM: Deborah Zemke Illustration, Sacramento, California

DESIGNER/ILLUSTRATOR: Deborah Zemke

TYPOGRAPHY: Lithographics

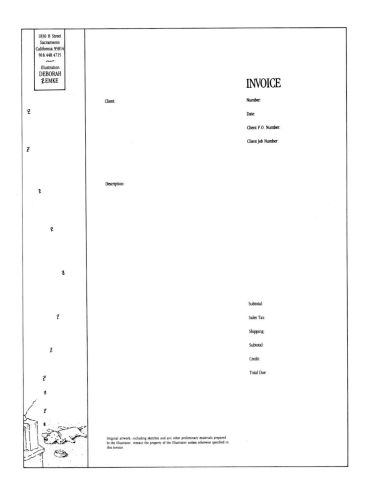

1830 H Street
Sacramento
California 95814
916.448.4715

Illustration
DEBORAH
ZEMKE

INVOICE

Client:

Description:

Number:

Date:

Client P.O. Number:

Client Job Number:

Subtotal:

Sales Tax:

Shipping:

Subtotal:

Credit:

Total Due:

Original artwork, including sketches and any other preliminary materials prepared by the Illustrator, remain the property of the Illustrator unless otherwise specified in this Invoice.

1830 H Street
Sacramento
California 95814
916.448.4715

Illustration
DEBORAH
ZEMKE

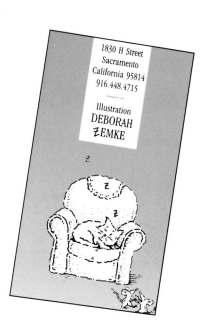

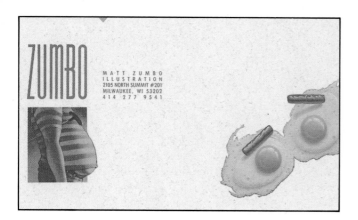

DESIGN FIRM: Thiel
Visual Design,
Milwaukee, Wisconsin
DESIGNER: Peter Tonn
ILLUSTRATOR: Matt
Zumbo

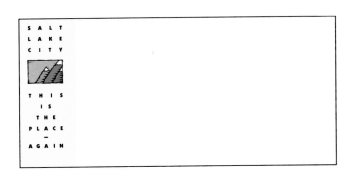

U.S. Mayors Conference

DESIGN FIRM: Cole &

Weber, Salt Lake

City, Utah

CREATIVE DIRECTOR:

Dave Newbold

DESIGNER: Steven Grigg

BRENDA WALTON
CALLIGRAPHY AND ILLUSTRATION
POST OFFICE BOX 161976
SACRAMENTO, CALIFORNIA 95816
TELEPHONE: 916.456.5833

Brenda Walton Calligraphy and Illustration

DESIGN FIRM: Brenda Walton Calligraphy and Illustration, Sacramento, California

DESIGNER/ILLUSTRATOR: Brenda Walton

BRENDA WALTON
CALLIGRAPHY AND ILLUSTRATION
POST OFFICE BOX 161976
SACRAMENTO, CALIFORNIA 95816
TELEPHONE: 916.456.5833

DESIGNER/ILLUSTRATOR:

Teddie Barnhart,

Germantown, Maryland

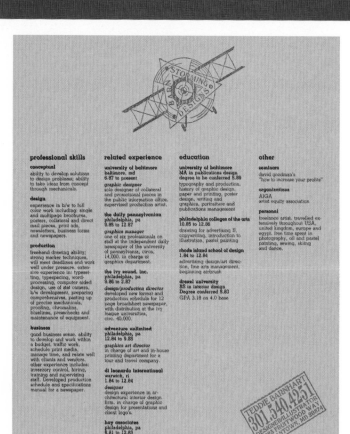

professional skills

conceptual
ability to develop solutions to design problems; ability to take ideas from concept through mechanicals.

design
experience in b/w to full color work including: single and multipage brochures, posters, collateral and direct mail pieces, print ads, newsletters, business forms and newspapers.

production
freehand drawing ability; strong marker techniques, will meet deadlines and work well under pressure, extensive experience in: typesetting, typespecing, word-processing, computer aided design, use of stat camera, b/w development, preparing comprehensives, pasting up of precise mechanicals, proofing, chromaline, bluelines, presschecks and maintenance of equipment.

business
good business sense, ability to develop and work within a budget, traffic work, schedule print media, manage time, and relate well with clients and vendors. other experience includes: inventory control, hiring, training and supervising staff. Developed production schedule and specifications manual for a newspaper.

related experience

university of baltimore
baltimore, md
6.87 to present
graphic designer
sole designer of collateral and promotional pieces in the public information office. supervised production artist.

the daily pennsylvanian
philadelphia, pa
9.85 to 12.87
graphics manager
one of six professionals on staff at the independent daily newspaper of the university of pennsylvania, circa, 14,000. in charge of graphics department.

the ivy sound, inc.
philadelphia, pa
9.86 to 2.87
design/production director
developed new format and production schedule for 12 page broadsheet newspaper, with distribution at the ivy league universities, circ. 40,000.

adventure unlimited
philadelphia, pa
12.84 to 9.85
graphics art director
in charge of art and in-house printing department for a tour and travel company.

di leonardo international
warwick, ri
1.84 to 12.84
designer
design experience in architectural interior design firm. in charge of graphic design for presentations and client logo's.

hay associates
philadelphia, pa
8.81 to 12.83
chartist
production experience in large corporate art department.

education

university of baltimore
MA in publications design degree to be conferred 8.89
typography and production, history of graphic design, paper and printing, poster design, writing and graphics, portraiture and publications management

philadelphia colleges of the arts
10.85 to 12.86
drawing for advertising II, copywriting, introduction to illustration, pastel painting

rhode island school of design
1.84 to 12.84
advertising design/art direction, fine arts management, beginning airbrush

drexel university
BS in interior design
Degree conferred 8.83
GPA 3.18 on 4.0 base

other

seminars
david goodman's "how to increase your profits"

organizations
AIGA
artist equity association

personal
freelance artist, travelled extensively throughout USA, united kingdom, europe and egypt. free time spent in photography, oil and pastel painting, sewing, skiing and dance.

MYRON GROSSMAN • 8800 Venice Blvd. • Los Angeles, CA • 90034 • (213) 559-9349

Invoice

To: _____

Date _____
Purchase Order # _____
Job # _____
Client _____

Description: _____

Itemized Expenses (Other Billable Items) _____

Subtotal _____
Sales Tax _____
Invoice # _____
Total _____

Myron Grossman Illustration

DESIGN FIRM: Myron Grossman Illustration, Pasadena, California
DESIGNER/ILLUSTRATOR: Myron Grossman

MYRON GROSSMAN

Illustration

213 ◆ 559-9349

8800 Venice Blvd ◆ LA, CA ◆ 90034

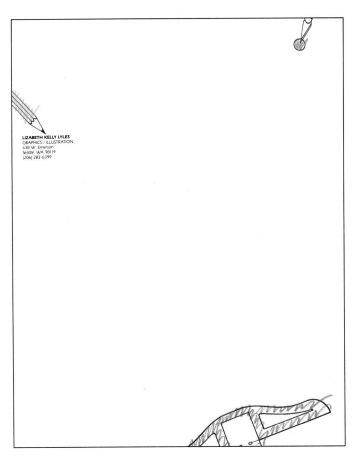

DESIGNER/ILLUSTRATOR:

Lizabeth Kelly Lyles,

Seattle, Washington

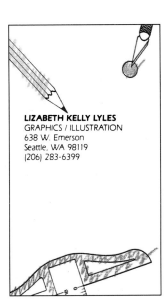

LIZABETH KELLY LYLES
GRAPHICS / ILLUSTRATION
638 W. Emerson
Seattle, WA 98119
(206) 283-6399

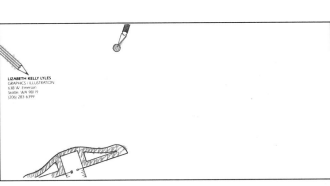

Lizabeth Kelly Lyles (Designer/Illustrator)

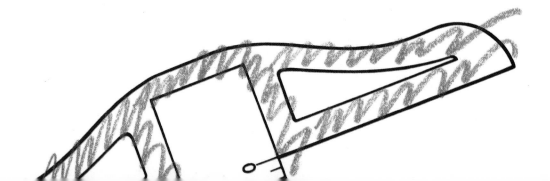

ROBIN SHEPHERD STUDIOS
DESIGN & MARKETING
FOUR SEVENTY-SIX RIVERSIDE
JACKSONVILLE, FLORIDA 32202
TELEPHONE (AREA 904) 359-0981

DESIGN FIRM: Robin

Shepherd Studios,

Jacksonville, Florida

CREATIVE DIRECTOR:

Robin Shepherd

ART DIRECTOR/

DESIGNER: Tom Nuijens

ILLUSTRATOR: Gerry

Bulgrin

ROBIN SHEPHERD STUDIOS
DESIGN & MARKETING
FOUR SEVENTY-SIX RIVERSIDE
JACKSONVILLE, FLORIDA 32202
TELEPHONE (AREA 904) 359-0981

TOM NUIJENS
ART DIRECTOR

ROBIN SHEPHERD STUDIOS
D E S I G N   &   M A R K E T I N G

FOUR SEVENTY-SIX RIVERSIDE
JACKSONVILLE, FLORIDA 32202
TELEPHONE (AREA 904) 359-0981

Robin Shepherd Studios (Design Firm)

Phone (916) 483-1957

7310 Fair Oaks Boulevard
Carmichael, California 95608

DESIGN FIRM: The Dunlavey Studio, Sacramento, California
ART DIRECTOR: Michael Dunlavey
DESIGNER: Lindy Dunlavey

7310 Fair Oaks Boulevard, Carmichael, Calif. 95608

Fabulous Fifties cafe

Sold to _____ For _____

Amount _____ Date _____

To

From

MOOLA

Value _____

Redeemable for food or merchandise only at the Fabulous Fifties Cafe, 7310 Fair Oaks Boulevard, Carmichael, CA, in the dollar amount shown on the face of this certificate. Valid for three months from date indicated. This certificate is non-transferable.

Fifties cafe

Kim Marlett

Phone 483-1957

7310 Fair Oaks Blvd., Carmichael, Calif. 95608

TOM WEBORG

JAVA CITY
ROASTERS
OF FINE COFFEES

1800 Capitol Avenue
Sacramento, CA 95814
Phone (916) 444-JAVA
444-5282

1800 Capitol Avenue
Sacramento, CA 95814
Phone (916) 444-JAVA 444-5282

DESIGN FIRM: The

Dunlavey Studio,

Sacramento, California

ART DIRECTOR: Michael

Dunlavey

DESIGNER: Lindy

Dunlavey

Java City (Coffee Roasters)

DESIGN FIRM: Ray
Sturdivant Graphic
Design, Dallas, Texas
DESIGNER/ILLUSTRATOR:
Ray Sturdivant

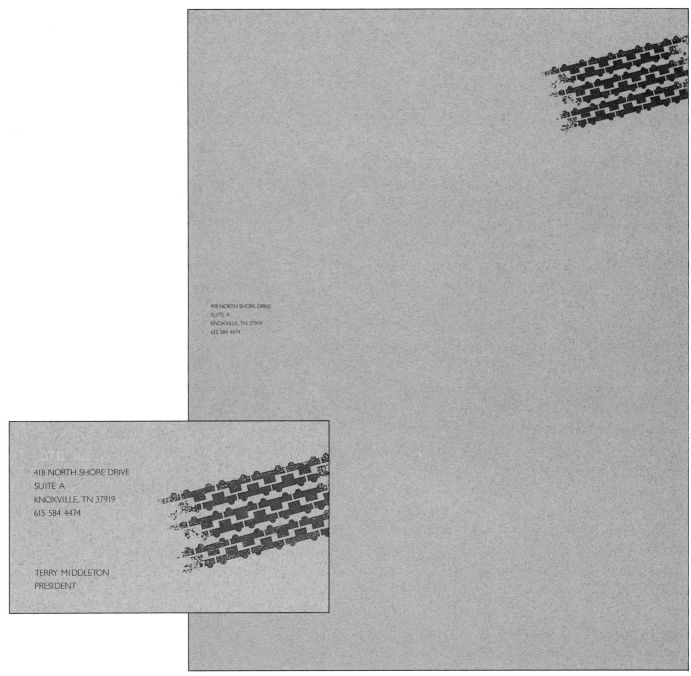

418 NORTH SHORE DRIVE
SUITE A
KNOXVILLE, TN 37919
615 584 4474

418 NORTH SHORE DRIVE
SUITE A
KNOXVILLE, TN 37919
615 584 4474

TERRY MIDDLETON
PRESIDENT

Lot of Autos

MICHAEL WOLK
DESIGN

4265
BRAGANZA
STREET

COCONUT GROVE
FLORIDA
33133

305. 662. 3031

DESIGN FIRM: Michael

Wolk Design,

Coconut Grove, Florida
DESIGNER: Michael Wolk

Michael Wolk Design

MICHAEL WOLK
DESIGN

4265
BRAGANZA
STREET

COCONUT GROVE
FLORIDA
33133

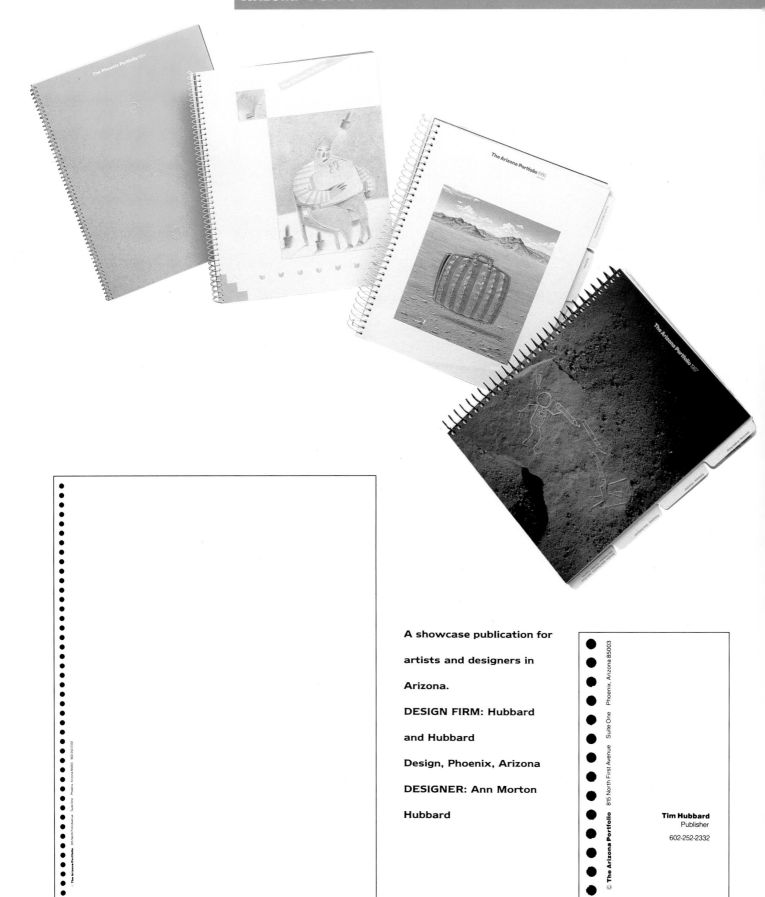

A showcase publication for
artists and designers in
Arizona.
DESIGN FIRM: Hubbard
and Hubbard
Design, Phoenix, Arizona
DESIGNER: Ann Morton
Hubbard

Tim Hubbard
Publisher
602-252-2332

© **The Arizona Portfolio** 815 North First Avenue   Suite One   Phoenix, Arizona 85003

© The Arizona Portfolio   815 North First Avenue   Suite One   Phoenix, Arizona 85003   602-252-2332

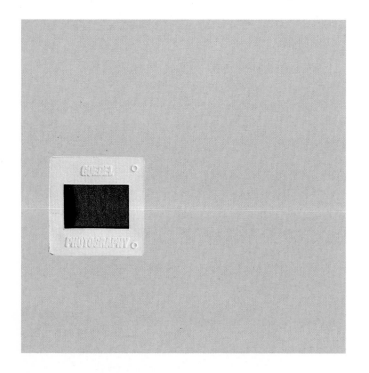

Brad Goebel

GOEBEL PHOTOGRAPHY
P.O. Box 552
217 W. Central
Andover, Kansas 67002
Telephone 316 733 0670

DESIGN FIRM: Gardner's

Graphic Hands,

Wichita, Kansas

DESIGNER: Bill Gardner

GOEBEL PHOTOGRAPHY, P.O. Box 552, 217 W. Central, Andover, Kansas 67002, Telephone 316 733 0670

DESIGN FIRM: Tyler A. Blik Design, San Diego, California

DESIGNERS: Tyler Blik, Gale Spitzley

PRODUCTION: Gale Spitzley

TYPOGRAPHY: Thompson Type

Mildred Love, A.I.A.

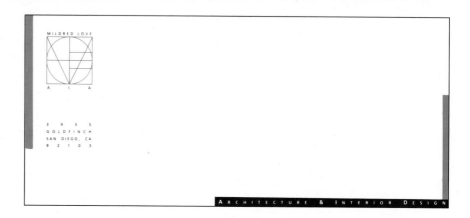

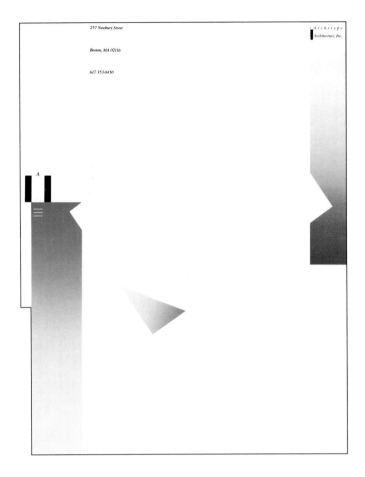

DESIGN FIRM: Skolos

Wedell + Raynor,

Inc., Charlestown,

Massachusetts

DESIGNER: Nancy Skolos

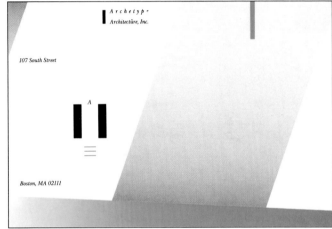

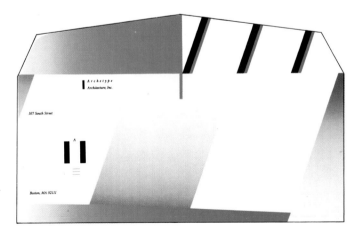

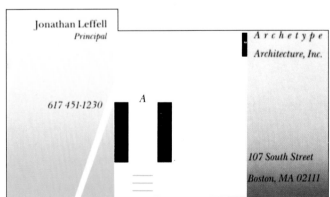

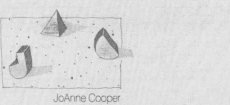

JoAnne Cooper

Date
Job No.
Client
Contact
Purchase Order No.

Description

Sales Tax

Terms Net 30 Days

2842 St Paul St
Baltimore MD 21218
(301) 366-2661

JoAnne Cooper

2842 St Paul St
Baltimore MD 21218
(301) 366-2661

DESIGN FIRM:

CooperWingard Design,

Baltimore, Maryland

DESIGNER/ILLUSTRATOR:

JoAnne Cooper

JoAnne Cooper

2842 St Paul St
Baltimore MD 21218

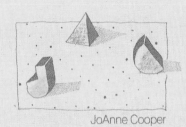

JoAnne Cooper

2842 St Paul St
Baltimore MD 21218
(301) 366-2661

DESIGN FIRM: Christina

Conte Advertising/

Design, Seattle,

Washington

DESIGNER: Christina

Conte

ILLUSTRATOR: Charlene

Tseng, Canoga Park,

California

CALLIGRAPHER: Tanya

Boldt

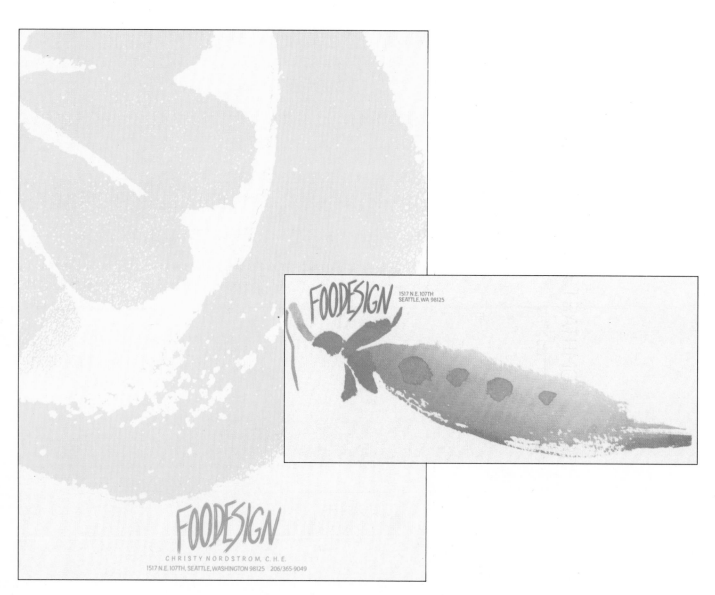

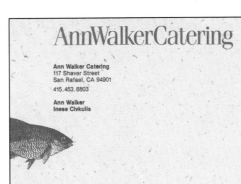

AnnWalkerCatering

Ann Walker Catering
117 Shaver Street
San Rafael, CA 94901

415.453.6803

Ann Walker
Inese Civkulis

AnnWalkerCatering

Ann Walker Catering
117 Shaver Street
San Rafael, CA 94901

DESIGN FIRM: Napoles &

Associates,

Kentfield, California

DESIGNER: Veronica

Napoles

TYPOGRAPHY: Hillside

Setting

Ann Walker Catering

AnnWalkerCatering

Ann Walker
Inese Civkulis

Ann Walker Catering
117 Shaver Street
San Rafael, CA 94901

415.453.6803

SEYMOUR ZIMBLER, M.D.

993 WATERTOWN STREET P.O. BOX 27 WEST NEWTON, MA 02165

DESIGN FIRM: Sondra

Zimble Design,

Wellesley, Massachusetts

DESIGNER/ILLUSTRATOR:

Sondra Zimble

SEYMOUR ZIMBLER, M.D.

PEDIATRIC ORTHOPEDICS
SURGERY OF THE SPINE

993 WATERTOWN STREET P.O. BOX 27
WEST NEWTON, MA 02165
(617) 527-7640

SEYMOUR ZIMBLER, M.D.

PEDIATRIC ORTHOPEDICS
SURGERY OF THE SPINE

993 WATERTOWN STREET P.O. BOX 27
WEST NEWTON, MA 02165

SEYMOUR ZIMBLER, M.D.
PEDIATRIC ORTHOPEDICS
SURGERY OF THE SPINE
993 WATERTOWN STREET P.O. BOX 27
WEST NEWTON, MA 02165
(617) 527-7640

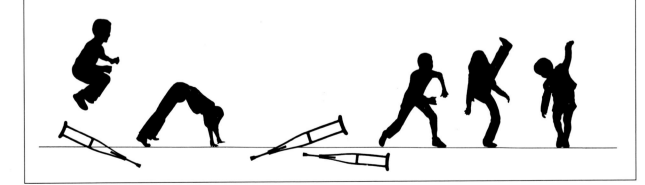

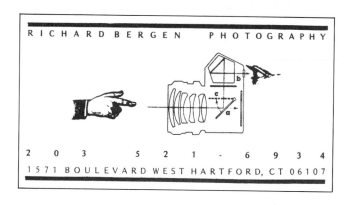

ART DIRECTOR/

DESIGNER: Tracy Lawlor,

Hartford, Connecticut

Richard Bergen Photography

Texas Hotel

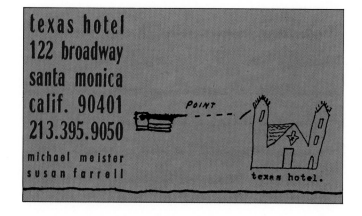

DESIGN FIRM:

Independent Project

Press, Los Angeles,

California

ART DIRECTOR: Michael

Meister

DESIGNER: Bruce Licher

ILLUSTRATOR: Michael

Stipe

UNIQUE HANDMADE
ORNAMENTS

DOUGH ART
1703 PEBBLE BROOK
O'FALLON, MO 63366
314-272-6505

SUE VANDERBILT
PROPRIETOR

A retailer of handmade

ornaments.

DESIGN FIRM: Obata-

Kuechner, Inc.,

St. Louis, Missouri

ART DIRECTOR: Kiku

Obata

DESIGNER/ILLUSTRATOR:

Ed Mantels-Seeker

Dough Art

N E A T S E A T S

Fine Upholstery. Beth Dupuis (512) 453-3719

Neat Seats (Furniture Upholstering)

DESIGN FIRM: Darnell

Design, Austin, Texas

DESIGNER/ILLUSTRATOR:

Tom Darnell

DESIGN FIRM: Collins

Design Group,

Lexington, Massachusetts

ART DIRECTOR/

DESIGNER: Brian Collins

TYPOGRAPHY: WordTech,

Inc.

Real Art Ways

94 Allyn Street
Hartford, CT 06103 1402
203 525 5521

A center for performance
and exhibition of
contemporary and
experimental art forms.
**DESIGN FIRM: Appleton
Design, Hartford,
Connecticut
DESIGNER: Robert
Appleton
TYPOGRAPHER:
Typographic House**

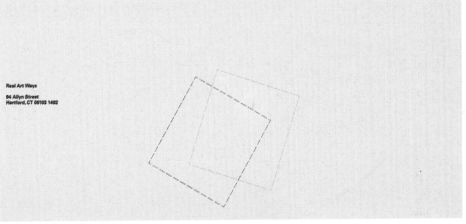

Real Art Ways

94 Allyn Street
Hartford, CT 06103 1402

Real Art Ways

K a r e n   W e i t z   P r o d u c t i o n s , I n c .

500 Fifth Avenue
New York, New York 10110
212-840-6626 Telex 221760

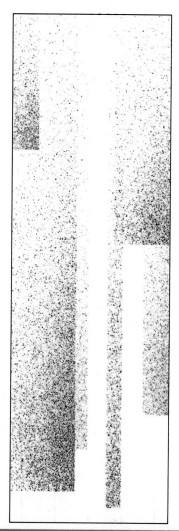

Karen Weitz Productions (Corporate Meeting Planner)

500 Fifth Avenue
New York, New York 10110

K a r e n   W e i t z   P r o d u c t i o n s , I n c .

DESIGN FIRM: Weisz Yang Dunkelberger, Inc., Westport, Connecticut
DESIGNER: David Dunkelberger

DESIGN FIRM: The Weller Institute for the Cure of Design, Park City, Utah
DESIGNER/ILLUSTRATOR: Don Weller

MUSIC OF THE SPHERES

MUSICUM LAUDE

2988 Avenel Terrace, Los Angeles, CA 90039 213-660-5444 Telex 6502653981

MUSIC OF THE SPHERES

MUSICUM LAUDE

Paul F. Antonelli

6431 Primrose Ave.
Suite 4
Los Angeles CA 90068
213-463-2162
Telex 6502653981

MUSIC OF THE SPHERES

MUSICUM LAUDE

GRAPHIC
SOLUTIONS

7604 BURHOLME AVE.
PHILA., PA 19111
(215) 722-1105

GRAPHIC
SOLUTIONS

7604 BURHOLME AVE.
PHILA., PA 19111

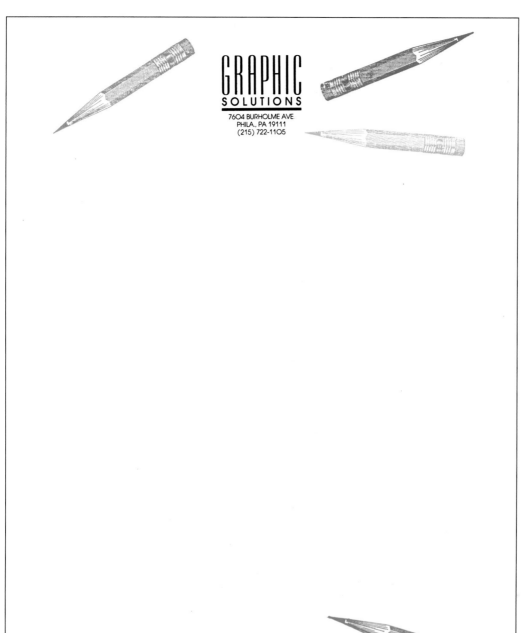

DESIGN FIRM: Graphic Solutions, Ardsley, Pennsylvania

DESIGNERS: Lenore Zekanis, Matthew Suchanec

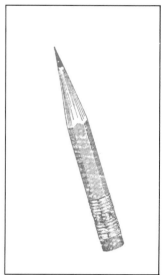

119

NORTH

FOURTH

STREET

SUITE 202

MINNEAPOLIS

MINNESOTA

55401

TELEPHONE:

612-338-3603

119

NORTH

FOURTH

STREET

SUITE 202

MINNEAPOLIS

MINNESOTA

55401

119   MINNEAPOLIS

NORTH   MINNESOTA

FOURTH   55401

STREET   TELÉPHONE:

SUITE 202   612-332-2603

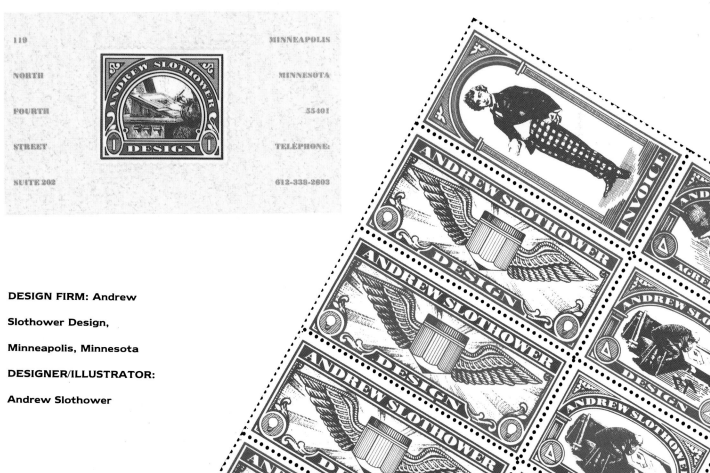

DESIGN FIRM: Andrew
Slothower Design,
Minneapolis, Minnesota
DESIGNER/ILLUSTRATOR:
Andrew Slothower

One CHILDREN's square,
Indianapolis, Indiana
46223

DESIGN FIRM: Design
Solutions,
Indianapolis, Indiana
ART DIRECTORS: David
Lesh, Ellen J. Sickle
DESIGNER: Ellen J. Sickle
ILLUSTRATOR: Alan E.
Cober

Riley Hospital for Children

B.D. FOX & FRIENDS, INC.
ADVERTISING
1111 BROADWAY
SANTA MONICA, CA 90401
213-394-7150

DESIGN FIRM: B.D. Fox &

Friends, Inc., Santa Monica,

California

ART DIRECTOR: Brian D.

Fox

DESIGNER: Robert Biro

PHOTOGRAPHER: Ron

Derhacopian

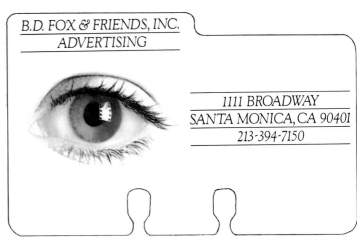

A firm specializing in venture capital for healthcare concerns.

DESIGN FIRM: Duffy Design Group, Minneapolis, Minnesota

ART DIRECTOR: Charles Spencer Anderson

DESIGNERS: Charles Spencer Anderson, Sharon Werner

ILLUSTRATORS: Charles Spencer Anderson, Lynn Schulte

Medical Innovation Capital, Inc.

MEDICAL

INNOVATION

PARTNERS

VENTURE

CAPITAL

LIMITED

PARTNERSHIPS

OPUS CENTER

SUITE 421

9900 BREN

ROAD EAST

MINNEAPOLIS

MINNESOTA

5 5 3 4 3

612•931•0154

FAX NUMBER

612•931•0003

M I C I

MEDICAL

INNOVATION

CAPITAL INC

TWELVE•O•ONE

MARQUETTE

AVENUE

MINNEAPOLIS

MINNESOTA

5 5 4 0 3

612•332•5130

Garry C. Buck
Designer / Illustrator
7501 N.W. 116th
Oklahoma City, OK 73132
405 • 721 • 3328

Garry C. Buck
Designer / Illustrator
7501 N.W. 116th
Oklahoma City, OK 73132
405 • 721 • 3328

DESIGNER/ILLUSTRATOR:

Gary C. Buck,

Oklahoma City, Oklahoma

S T A T E M E N T

Job # _____

Client _____ Date _____

Address _____

Job Title / Description _____

Description & specs of work now authorized:

Garry C. Buck
Designer / Illustrator
7501 N.W. 116th
Oklahoma City, OK 73132
405 • 721 • 3328

Garry C. Buck
Designer / Illustrator
7501 N.W. 116th
Oklahoma City, OK 73132
405 • 721 • 3328

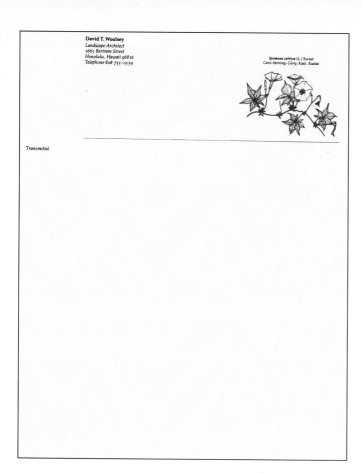

David T. Woolsey
Landscape Architect
1665 Bertram Street
Honolulu, Hawaii 96816
Telephone 808 735-0539

Ipomoea cairica (L.) Sweet
Cairo Morning-Glory: Koali, Koaliai

Transmittal

David T. Woolsey
Landscape Architect
1665 Bertram Street
Honolulu, Hawaii 96816
Telephone 808 735-0539

Pteralyxia macrocarpa (Hillebr.) K. Schum.
Ridged Pteralyxia, Kaulu

Invoice

DESIGNER: Bud

Linschoten, Honolulu,

Hawaii

David T. Woolsey, Landscape Architect

David T. Woolsey
Landscape Architect
1665 Bertram Street
Honolulu, Hawaii 96816
Telephone 808 735-0539

Ipomoea tuboides Degener and Van Ooststr
Hawaiian Moonflower

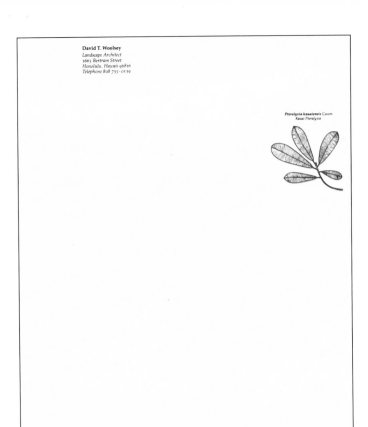

David T. Woolsey
Landscape Architect
1665 Bertram Street
Honolulu, Hawaii 96816
Telephone 808 735-0539

Pteralyxia kauaiensis Caum
Kauai Pteralyxia

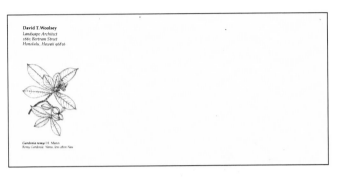

David T. Woolsey
Landscape Architect
1665 Bertram Street
Honolulu, Hawaii 96816

Gardenia remyi H. Mann
Remy Gardenia; Nanu, less often Nau

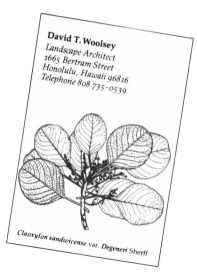

David T. Woolsey
Landscape Architect
1665 Bertram Street
Honolulu, Hawaii 96816
Telephone 808 735-0539

Claoxylon sandwicense var. *Degeneri* Sherff

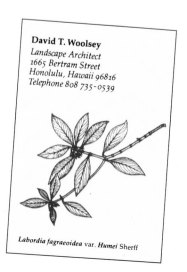

David T. Woolsey
Landscape Architect
1665 Bertram Street
Honolulu, Hawaii 96816
Telephone 808 735-0539

Labordia fagraeoidea var. *Humei* Sherff

David T. Woolsey
Landscape Architect
1665 Bertram Street
Honolulu, Hawaii 96816
Telephone 808 735-0539

Acacia koaia Hilleb.
Dwarf Koa: Akoa, Koaie

Peek (pē·k) *noun* The summit. The highest point. The top. As in Lori Adamski-Peek.   Photographer.

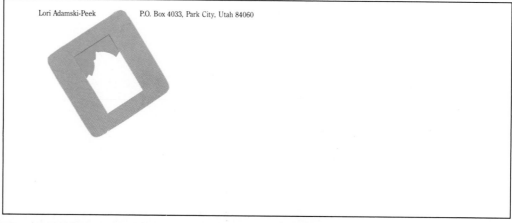

Lori Adamski-Peek   P.O. Box 4033, Park City, Utah 84060   (801) 649-0259

Lori Adamski-Peek   P.O. Box 4033, Park City, Utah 84060

DESIGN FIRM: Weller Institute for the Cure of Design, Park City, Utah

DESIGNER/ILLUSTRATOR: Don Weller

Lori Adamski Peek (Photographer)

DESIGN FIRM: The Weller Institute for the Cure of Design, Park City, Utah
DESIGNER/ILLUSTRATOR: Don Weller

letterhead

Lodestar Productions Inc. Visual Communications
9606 Heather Road · Beverly Hills, California 90210

213·275·3288

Lodestar Productions, Inc.

business card

213-275-3288

Lodestar Productions Inc. Visual Communications
9606 Heather Road · Beverly Hills, California 90210

DESIGN FIRM: Lodestar Productions, Inc., Beverly Hills, California
DESIGNER: Barry Feinstein

envelope

Lodestar Productions Inc Visual Communications
9606 Heather Road · Beverly Hills, California 90210

mailing label

Lodestar Productions Inc Visual Communications
9606 Heather Road · Beverly Hills, California 90210

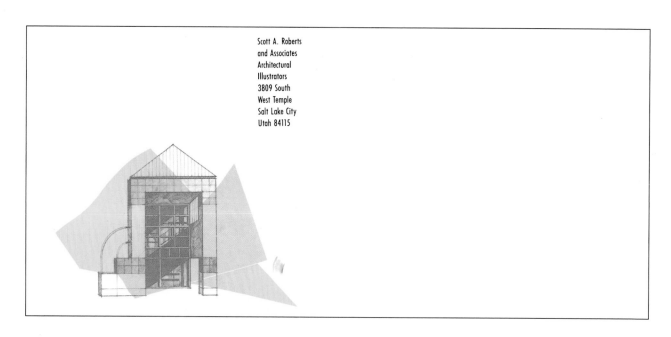

Scott A. Roberts
and Associates
Architectural
Illustrators
3809 South
West Temple
Salt Lake City
Utah 84115

Scott A. Roberts

Scott A. Roberts
and Associates
Architectural
Illustrators
3809 South
West Temple
Salt Lake City
Utah 84115
(801) 268-0483

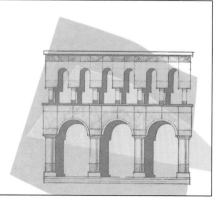

DESIGN FIRM: Kira Kilmer

Design,

Salt Lake City, Utah

DESIGNER: Kira Kilmer

ILLUSTRATOR: Scott

Roberts

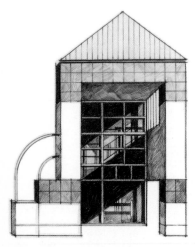

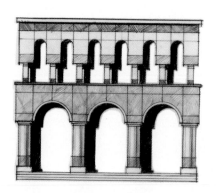

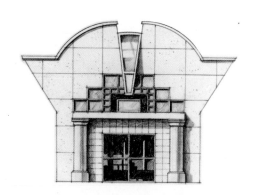

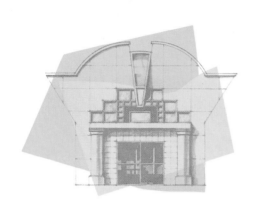

Scott A. Roberts
and Associates
Architectural
Illustrators
3809 South
West Temple
Salt Lake City
Utah 84115
(801) 268-0483

Rose DeNeve
Copywriter

171 East 77 Street
New York, NY 10021

212 249 0316

DESIGN FIRM: Cook and

Shanosky Associates,

Inc., Princeton, New Jersey

ART DIRECTORS: Roger

Cook, Don Shanosky

DESIGNERS: Roger Cook,

Don Shanosky, Rob

Frankle

TYPOGRAPHY: Tristin, Inc.

Rose DeNeve (Copywriter)

Rose DeNeve
Copywriter

171 East 77 Street
New York, NY 10021

212 249 0316

634 BRANNAN ST.

SAN FRANCISCO

CALIFORNIA

94107

PHONE 415 • 986 • 7740

FAX 415 • 543 • 5454

A national chain of
wholesale flower
markets.

**DESIGN FIRM: Eric Shalit
Designs, Seattle,
Washington**

**DESIGNER/ILLUSTRATOR:
Eric Shalit**

Sunflor

DESIGN FIRM: Peter Taflan

Marketing

Communications, Durham,

North Carolina

CREATIVE DIRECTOR:

Peter Taflan

DESIGNER: Charlotte

White

Fire Suppression
Technologies, Inc.

1409 Imperial Drive
Durham, NC 27712
919/383-5324
919/471-3537

Fire Suppression
Technologies, Inc.

1409 Imperial Drive
Durham, NC 27712
919/471-3537
919/383-5324

Stan Parker

Commercial & Industrial
Fire Training
Fire & Safety Equipment
Sales & Service

601

Munroe Street

Sacramento

CA 95825

Lemon Grass Restaurant

DESIGN FIRM: The

Dunlavey Studio,

Sacramento, California

ART DIRECTOR: Michael

Dunlavey

DESIGNER: Lindy

Dunlavey

LEMON GRASS
Restaurant

601

Munroe Street

Sacramento

CA 95825

(916) 486-4891

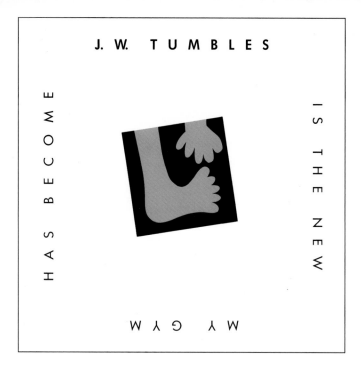

J. W. TUMBLES

HAS BECOME

IS THE NEW

MY GYM

J.W. TUMBLES

A Children's Gym
140 South Solana Hills Drive
Plaza West II Shopping Center
Solana Beach, California 92075
619-481-5576

DESIGN FIRM: Richardson

or Richardson,

Phoenix, Arizona

ART DIRECTORS: Forrest

Richardson,

Valerie Richardson

DESIGNER: Rosemary

Connelly

TYPOGRAPHY: DigiType

Jeffrey Woods
Director

J.W. TUMBLES

A Children's Gym
140 South Solana Hills Drive
Plaza West II Shopping Center
Solana Beach, California 92075
619-481-5576

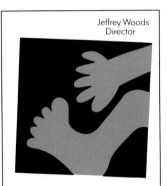

Jeffrey Woods
Director

J.W. TUMBLES

A Children's Gym
140 South Solana Hills Drive
Plaza West II Shopping Center
Solana Beach, California 92075
619-481-5576

TUMBLEWEED.

DESIGN FIRM: Michael
Brock Design,
Los Angeles, California
ART DIRECTOR: Michael
Brock
DESIGNER: Gaylen Braun
PHOTOGRAPHER: Tom
Keller

TUMBLEWEED

190 SOUTH BEVERLY DRIVE BEVERLY HILLS CA 90212 274·5844

DESIGN FIRM: Jacomini &
Duda Design & Illustration,
Bowling Green, Ohio
ART DIRECTORS/
DESIGNERS: Ronald
Jacomini, Tony Duda
ILLUSTRATOR: Tony Duda

Jacomini & Duda Design & Illustration

PROPS

LOCATIONS

FOOD
STYLIST

JANICE (JANA) BLUE
1708 ROSEWOOD
HOUSTON, TEXAS 77004

(713) 522-6899

PHOTO STYLIST &
TV PRODUCTION SERVICES

DESIGN FIRM: Loucks
Atelier, Inc.,
Houston, Texas
DESIGNER/ILLUSTRATOR:
Doug Gobel

LOCATIONS

PROPS

1708 ROSEWOOD
HOUSTON, TEXAS 77004

FOOD
STYLIST

CASTING &

WARDROBE

CASTING &

WARDROBE

PROPS

JANICE (JANA) BLUE
1708 ROSEWOOD
HOUSTON, TEXAS 77004

(713) 522-6899

PHOTO STYLIST &
TV PRODUCTION SERVICES

FOOD

STYLIST

JANICE (JANA) BLUE
1708 ROSEWOOD
HOUSTON, TEXAS 77004

(713) 522-6899

PHOTO STYLIST &
TV PRODUCTION SERVICES

Janice Blue, Photo Stylist

DESIGN FIRM: Rubin

Cordaro Design,

Minneapolis, Minnesota

ART DIRECTOR: Bruce

Rubin

DESIGNER: William

Homan

TYPOGRAPHY: P&H Photo

Composition

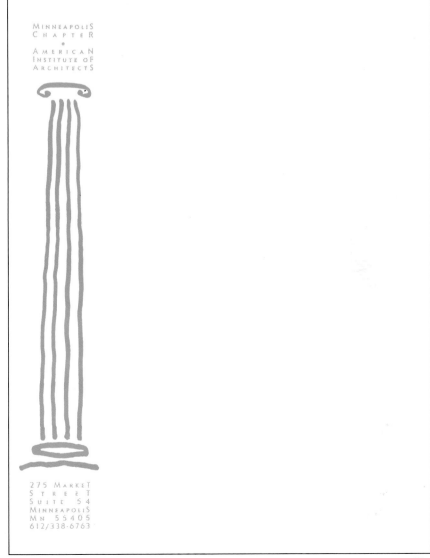

DESIGN FIRM: Sue Crolick

Advertising & Design,

Minneapolis, Minnesota

DESIGNER: Sue Crolick

PHOTOGRAPHER: Joe

Giannetti

KEYLINER: Nancy Johnson

TYPOGRAPHY: Great

Faces

GIANNETTI PHOTOGRAPHY
127 N. Seventh Street, Suite 402
Minneapolis, MN 55403 (612) 339-3172

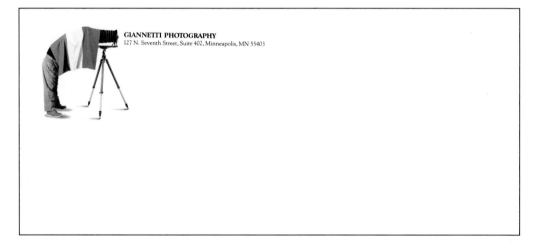

GIANNETTI PHOTOGRAPHY
127 N. Seventh Street, Suite 402, Minneapolis, MN 55403

GIANNETTI PHOTOGRAPHY
127 N. Seventh Street, Suite 402
Minneapolis, MN 55403 (612) 339-3172

Giannetti Photography

GIANNETTI PHOTOGRAPHY
127 N. Seventh Street, Suite 402, Minneapolis, MN 55403 (612) 339-3172

Marianne

G
L
A
D
Y
C
H

Design

1814 Thayer Avenue / Los Angeles California 90025 / 213 474 1915

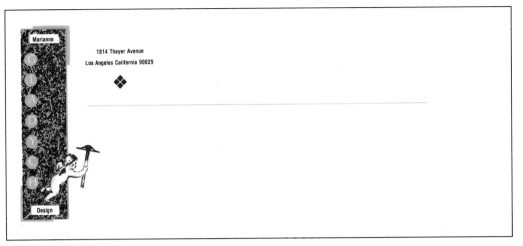

1814 Thayer Avenue
Los Angeles California 90025

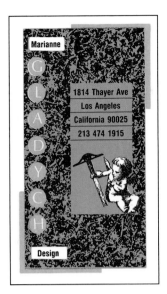

Marianne

GLADYCH

1814 Thayer Ave
Los Angeles
California 90025
213 474 1915

Design

Marianne

GLADYCH

A Special
Presentation

Design

for:

DESIGN FIRM: Marianne

Gladych Design,

Los Angeles, California

DESIGNER/ILLUSTRATOR:

Marianne Gladych

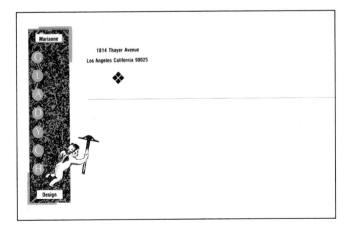

Marianne

GLADYCH

1814 Thayer Avenue
Los Angeles California 90025

Design

DESIGN FIRM: Wilson

Creative Services,

San Diego, California

ART DIRECTOR/

DESIGNER: Daniel C.

Wilson

ILLUSTRATORS: Daniel C.

Wilson, Julian Naranjo

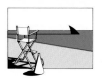

FROM THE DESK OF
RICHARD SANDS

RICHARD SANDS PRODUCTIONS 18901 VIEW CREST DRIVE SONOMA, CA 95476 (707) 996-7159

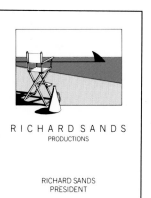

RICHARD SANDS
PRODUCTIONS

RICHARD SANDS
PRESIDENT

18901 VIEW CREST DRIVE
SONOMA, CA 95476 (707) 996-7159

Richard Sands Productions (Film Producer)

RICHARD SANDS
PRODUCTIONS

DESIGNER/ILLUSTRATOR: State College,

Lanny Sommese,   Pennsylvania

**CATHY
ZANGRILLI**
WIFE
MOM
ART LOVER
DESIGNER
BALLOONIST
500
WEST
FAIRMOUNT
AVENUE
STATE
COLLEGE
PENNSYLVANIA
16801
(814)
237
2838

DESIGN FIRM: PriceWeber

Marketing

Communications, Inc.,

Louisville, Kentucky

CREATIVE DIRECTOR:

Larry A. Profancik

DESIGNER: Juan Lopez-

Bonilla

ILLUSTRATOR: Dave

Fields

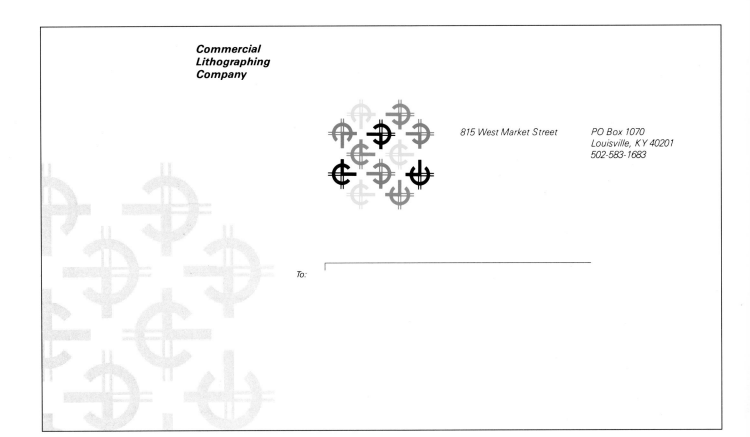

Commercial Lithographing Company

815 West Market Street

PO Box 1070
Louisville, KY 40201
502-583-1683

To:

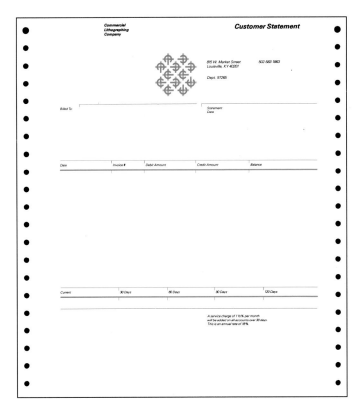

Commercial Lithographing Company

Customer Statement

815 W. Market Street
Louisville, KY 40201

502-583-1863

Dept. 97265

Billed To:

Statement
Date

Date	Invoice #	Debit Amount	Credit Amount	Balance

Current	30 Days	60 Days	90 Days	120 Days

A service charge of 1½% per month
will be added on all accounts over 30 days.
This is an annual rate of 18%.

Commercial Lithographing Company

815 West Market Street

PO Box 1070
Louisville, KY 40201
502-583-1683

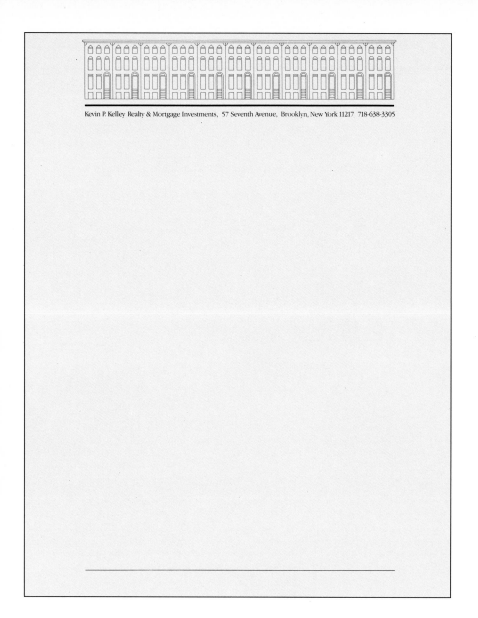

Kevin P. Kelley Realty & Mortgage Investments, 57 Seventh Avenue, Brooklyn, New York 11217 718-638-3305

DESIGN FIRM: Fisher

Design, Inc.,

New York, New York

DESIGNER/ILLUSTRATOR:

Jill Fisher

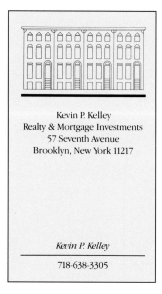

Kevin P. Kelley
Realty & Mortgage Investments
57 Seventh Avenue
Brooklyn, New York 11217

Kevin P. Kelley

718-638-3305

Kevin P. Kelly Realty and Mortgage Investments

Kevin P. Kelley
Realty & Mortgage Investments
57 Seventh Avenue
Brooklyn, New York 11217

Sharon Boguch (Location Scout)

DESIGN FIRM: W. Joseph Gagnon Design Associates, Seattle, Washington

DESIGNER: W. Joseph Gagnon

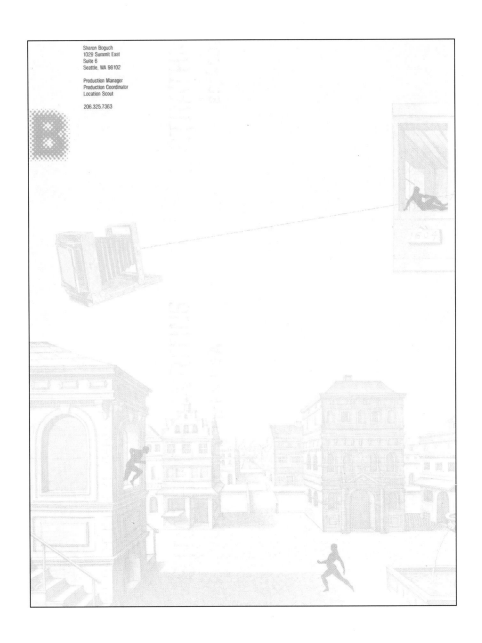

Rio de Janeiro

Ivac Corporation Sales Incentive Trip to Rio de Janeiro

DESIGN FIRM: Mires Design, Inc., San Diego, California
ART DIRECTOR/ DESIGNER: Scott Mires
PRODUCTION: Kathy Carpentier-Moore
ACCOUNT EXECUTIVE: Lisa Stewart

R I O   D E   J A N E I R O

FIRST DAY
THURSDAY, APRIL 23, 1987
Daytime/Evening Dress: Comfortable traveling clothes; overnight flight toiletries, magazines, etc.

Domestic Winners: Today you'll fly from your home cities to Miami. You'll meet your IVAC Travel Director at the Pan Am Ticket Counter at the Miami International Airport no later than 9:45 p.m. this evening. You'll need to present documentation for international check-in.

11:45 p.m. Pan Am flight #441 departs Miami for overnight flight to Rio de Janeiro.

International Winners: Today you will fly from your home cities to Rio de Janeiro. You will be met when you arrive in Rio by your IVAC Travel Staff (look for IVAC sign).

R I O   D E   J A N E I R O

SECOND DAY
FRIDAY, APRIL 24, 1987
Daytime Dress: Comfortable traveling clothes; sportswear for afternoon.

Evening Dress: Casual; slacks for men and cool sundress or slacks for ladies.

International winners arrive Rio early this morning. Please follow Airport Arrival Procedures listed below.

8:50 a.m. Domestic winners arrive in Rio. Please follow Airport Arrival Procedures listed below.

AIRPORT ARRIVAL PROCEDURES—
Upon disembarking the plane, proceed to Immigration. Here they will check your passport.

After passing through Immigration, you must retrieve your own luggage and proceed to Customs. Once you are outside the Customs area, look for your IVAC Travel Staff holding an IVAC sign. They will assist you with transportation to the Rio Palace.

Upon arrival at the Rio Palace, you'll check into the hotel and receive your Welcome Kit and name badge. Luggage will be sent directly to your room.

The rest of the day is yours to relax and unwind. Each person will receive a cash allowance for lunch today.

7:00 p.m. Join fellow IVAC winners poolside at the Rio Palace for a "Welcome to Rio" cocktail party featuring icy tropical libations, lavish buffet dinner and local entertainment.

R I O   D E   J A N E I R O

FIFTH DAY
MONDAY, APRIL 27, 1987
Daytime Dress: Sportswear.

Evening Dress: Colorful, casual "carioca" dress.

Today is yours to spend as you like. Begin with breakfast in the hotel. Remember to sign the check with your name, room number and IVAC.

One of Rio highlights . . . and great delights . . . are her gemstone houses. Two of the largest in Rio are H. Stern and Moreno. The Hospitality Desk can arrange for tours and transportation to either house for you.

Other activities you may enjoy include:
Golf
Tennis
Shopping
Beach Activities
Area Sightseeing

Please check with your Travel Staff if you need assistance.

Everyone will receive a cash allowance for lunch today.

6:30 p.m. This evening IVAC guests gather in the lobby, and then depart for the exclusive Rio Yacht Club for a festive "Carnival Party," including cocktails, delicious dinner and native entertainment with traditional samba music.

R I O   D E   J A N E I R O

SIXTH DAY
TUESDAY, APRIL 28, 1987
Daytime Dress: Sportswear.

Evening Dress: Casual.

Today is yours to explore Rio . . . from beach to shopping to sports activities. Your Travel Staff at the IVAC Hospitality Desk can arrange additional tours as well.

Each person will receive a cash allowance for lunch today.

Enjoy your day!

Dinner is at your leisure this evening (cash allowance) . . .

G E N E R A L   I N F O R M A T I O N

CURRENCY
The unit of currency in Rio is the Cruzado (Cz$). As of this writing, 17 Cz$ = $1.00 US. That means that one (1) Cruzado = $.06 U.S. The rate of exchange is quite good with most currencies; we suggest you pay for items in cruzados.

You may change money at the airport, hotel and banks. Banks are closed on weekends, and are open Monday–Friday, 10:00 a.m. to 4:30 p.m. The hotel can covert cash or traveller's checks for you any time. Most international credit cards are accepted at businesses, restaurants and hotels.

Important: When leaving Rio, you must change Cruzados back to your home country's currency. To do this, you must show your conversion receipts—please keep them in a safe place to avoid reconversion problems when leaving Brazil. Conversion can be done at the airport prior to departure. You can repurchase dollars only up to 30% of the amount cashed.

FOOD AND WATER
You are best advised to drink bottled water, beer and soft drinks. The general rule of thumb is you can eat anything that is boiled, cooked or peeled (including local fruit).

Local drinks like rum and beer (Brahma) are very good, as is the national drink called a "caipirinha"; made of sugar-cane liqueur, lime and sugar—very potent! Other specialties include "feijoada," a dish of black beans and pork, and churrasco, large pieces of beef, pork and other meats barbecued. Local seafood is also excellent.

Brazilians customarily dine quite late, around 9 or 10 p.m.; with this in mind, you might want to plan on a big lunch.

R I O   D E   J A N E I R O

EIGHTH DAY
THURSDAY, APRIL 30, 1987
Daytime Dress: Beachwear, bathing suit.

Evening Dress: Casual dinner attire.

Fire up!! Today's the Third Annual IVAC Olympics!!

8:00 a.m. Olympic Day begins with a "fire up" breakfast in a private room of the hotel (please check the Hospitality Desk for specific room).

9:00 a.m. Olympiads meet in the hotel lobby for transfer to the dock and private sail to the Ilha Martins. Once moored at the island, the events begin!

Olympiads enjoy a picnic lunch on the island.

Return is scheduled for approximately 5:00 p.m.

After a full day of competition, enjoy a well-deserved dinner on your own this evening (cash allowance provided).

MIKE SALISBURY
COMMUNICATIONS
2 2 0 0
AMAPOLA
COURT
TORRANCE, CA
9 0 5 0 1
213 320-7660

A & M Records
Akademos (WRG)
Baskin-Robbins (OEM)
Blue Note Records
Bodyboarding Magazine
Brittania Jeans (WRG)
Bud Light (Sante)
C & H Sugar (FCB Honig)
Cornels (McCann/Erickson)
CBS Fox Video
CBS/Columbia Records
Cheetah Shadow
Chevrolet (Yic Olesen)
Chrysler Corp.
City Magazine
Coco's Restaurants (DYR)
Columbia Pictures
Criswell Development Co.
D.E.G.
Disneyland
Dorman Winthrop
Embassy Pictures
Esquire
Fats Domino
Filmex
Frances Coppola
George Harrison
Giorgio
Gordon & Smith
Gotcha
Harper's Bazaar
Harry's Bar & American Grill
Hollywood Reporter
Jack in the Box (WRG)
James Taylor
Jerry Maguire
Keystone Resort (WRG)
Levi Strauss (FCB, Honig)
Life
Lincoln Mercury
London Sunday Times
Lorimar
Los Angeles Herald Examiner
Los Angeles Times
LucasFilm
Made in the Shade Jeans
Mattel Toys (OEM)
Medallion Books
MGM
Michael Jackson
Nalley Foods
National Endowment for the Arts
NBC
New Horizon Pictures
New World Pictures
Newport Publications
Newsweek
O'Neill
Ocean Pacific Sunwear, Ltd.
Orion Pictures
Paramount Pictures
Petersen Publishing
Playboy
Ponderosa Homes
Ralston-Purina (WRG)
Randy Newman
RCA
Revell Toys (DYR)
Rickie Lee Jones
Rolling Stone Magazine
San Francisco Examiner
Schick
Scotti Bros. Records
Sebastian International
Software Ventures
Standard Shoes
Straightarrow Books
Surfing Magazine
Tina Turner
Tri-Star Pictures
Twentieth Century Fox
U.S. Suzuki (DYR)
United Artists
Universal Studios
Vogue
Warner Bros. Pictures
Warner Bros. Records
Warner Home Video
White Water Falls (W.B. Doner)
ZEGN AM 95

DATE:

JOB #:

WRITER:

■ **MIKE SALISBURY COMMUNICATIONS** 2200 AMAPOLA CT TORRANCE CA 90501 213 320-7660

Mike Salisbury Communications (Design Firm)

DESIGN FIRM: Mike Salisbury Communications, Torrance, California

ART DIRECTOR: Michael Salisbury

DESIGNER: Cindy Luck

DESIGN FIRM: CBS Records, New York, New York

DESIGNER: Allen Weinberg

ILLUSTRATOR: Fred Swanson

DESIGN FIRM: Nancy

Davis Design,

Portland, Oregon

DESIGNER/ILLUSTRATOR:

Nancy Davis

Common Threads (Clothing Store for Adults)

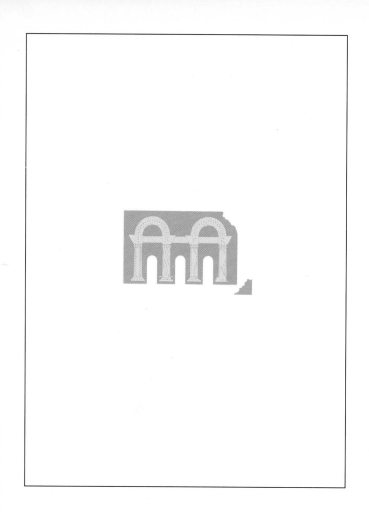

A research center
investigating the
safety risks of
different professions.
DESIGN FIRM: Barry Seifer
& Co., Ann Arbor, Michigan
CREATIVE DIRECTOR/
ILLUSTRATOR:
Barry Seifer
DESIGNERS: Barry Seifer,
Sharon Smentowski,
Karen Moeller

In 1985 thirteen concerned physicians, attorneys, and other interested professionals founded the non-profit Institute for the Study of Professional Risk (ISPR). We formed ISPR because we believe that professional liability has become a major political and social issue. We also believe that for too long the professions have been tainted by pejorative labeling of all their members, due to the negligence of a few. Society as a whole and the professions have suffered as a result of this attitude.

Institute for the Study of Professional Risk

INSTITUTE FOR THE STUDY OF PROFESSIONAL RISK

P.O. BOX 4224   ANN ARBOR, MICHIGAN 48106   313-668-1767

■ DOMINGO
■ GONZÁLEZ
■ DESIGN
ARCHITECTURAL
LIGHTING DESIGN
47 ANN STREET
NEW YORK NY 10038
■ PH 212 608 4800

- DOMINGO
- GONZALEZ
- DESIGN
ARCHITECTURAL
LIGHTING DESIGN
47 ANN STREET
NEW YORK NY 10038
- PH 212 608 4800

- DOMINGO
- GONZALEZ
- DESIGN
ARCHITECTURAL
LIGHTING DESIGN
47 ANN STREET
NEW YORK NY 10038
- PH 212 608 4800

TRANSMITTAL
Date: Enclosed:

To:

Attention:

Project:

Job Number:

Via:

cc: Comments:

By:

- DOMINGO
- GONZÁLEZ
- DESIGN
ARCHITECTURAL
LIGHTING DESIGN
47 ANN STREET
NEW YORK NY 10038
- PH 212 608 4800   Corinne Monnard

- DOMINGO
- GONZÁLEZ
- DESIGN
ARCHITECTURAL
LIGHTING DESIGN
47 ANN STREET
NEW YORK NY 10038

DESIGN FIRM: Perri

DeFino Graphic

Design, Astoria, New York

DESIGNER: Perri DeFino

Ron Lieser Design

DESIGN FIRM: Ron Lieser

Design,

Worthington, Ohio

DESIGNER: Ron Lieser

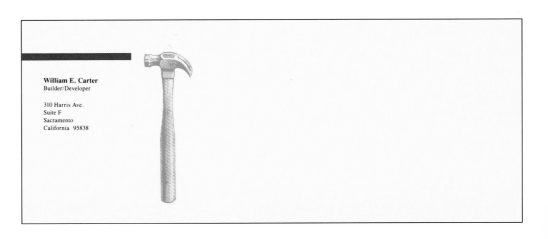

William E. Carter Construction

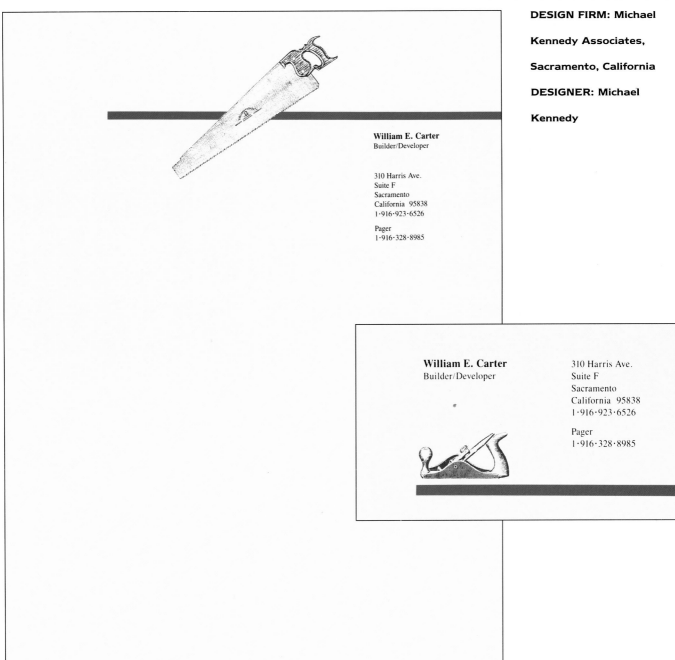

William E. Carter
Builder/Developer

310 Harris Ave.
Suite F
Sacramento
California 95838
1·916·923·6526

Pager
1·916·328·8985

William E. Carter
Builder/Developer

310 Harris Ave.
Suite F
Sacramento
California 95838
1·916·923·6526

Pager
1·916·328·8985

DESIGN FIRM: Michael Kennedy Associates, Sacramento, California
DESIGNER: Michael Kennedy

DESIGN FIRM: Robin Shepherd Studios, Jacksonville, Florida

ART DIRECTOR/ DESIGNER: Tom Schifanella

CALLIGRAPHER: Pamela Stanholtzer

PHOTOGRAPHER: Stuart Findlay

Native American Art

202 WHARFSIDE WAY
JACKSONVILLE, FLORIDA 32207
(904) 398-3677

Native American Art

Native American Art

Doris Gordy

202 WHARFSIDE WAY
JACKSONVILLE, FLORIDA 32207
(904) 398-3677

B'ARBARA WALKER

WINGS FASHION APPAREL COMPANY
2018 SAN MARCO BOULEVARD
JACKSONVILLE, FLORIDA 32207
904/398-1577

WINGS FASHION APPAREL COMPANY
2018 SAN MARCO BOULEVARD
JACKSONVILLE, FLORIDA 32207
904/398-1577

DESIGN FIRM: Robin
Shepherd Studios,
Jacksonville, Florida
ART DIRECTOR/
ILLUSTRATOR: Tom
Schifanella
DESIGNER: Tom Nuijens

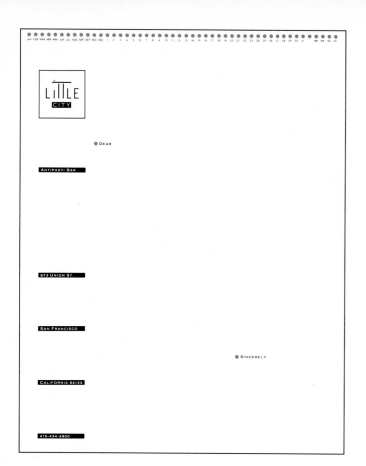

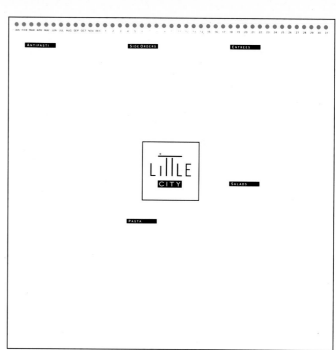

DESIGN FIRM: Bruce

Yelaska Design,

San Francisco, California

ART DIRECTOR/

DESIGNER: Bruce Yelaska

Little City Restaurant

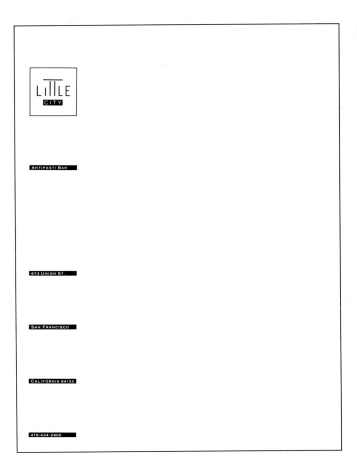

ANTIPASTI BAR

673 UNION ST.

SAN FRANCISCO

CALIFORNIA 94133

415-434-2900

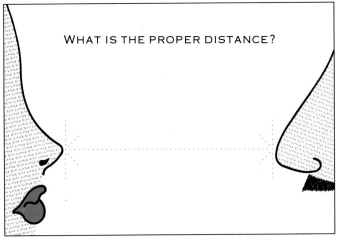

ANTIPASTI

GARLIC AND PANCETTA SOUP WITH TOASTED CROUTONS AND MELTED ASIAGO CHEESE...........4.50

MUSHROOMS RELLENOS (STUFFED WITH ASIAGO CHEESE, PIMIENTO & BREADCRUMBS)..........5.25

GRILLED EGGPLANT AND SMOKED MOZZARELLA WITH ROASTED BELL PEPPERS & CAPERS.........5.50

GRILLED GRAPE LEAVES STUFFED WITH PINE NUTS & FRESH & AGED GOAT CHEESE; SUN DRIED TOMATO VINAIGRETTE..........5.50

SPAGHETTI RAPIDO WITH GARLIC, CHILIS, PARSLEY AND EXTRA VIRGIN OLIVE OIL........6.25

KEFTA (MIDDLE EASTERN GROUND LAMB PATTIES) WITH CORIANDER-MINT YOGURT.............5.50

GRILLED, SKEWERED CHICKEN INDIENNE & MANGO CHUTNEY.5.75

MINI MIXED GRILL OF ITALIAN SAUSAGE, SPICY CHICKEN WINGS & SHRIMP BORRACHOS......7.25

GRILLED ITALIAN SAUSAGES (CALABRESE AND/OR TUSCANO) & BAKED POLENTA...........7.75

CLAMS AND MUSSELS STEAMED IN WHITE WINE, CILANTRO, GINGER AND ORANGE ZEST WITH SESAME-CHILIS AIOLI...........7.50

GRILLED SHRIMP BORRACHOS (IN THE SHELL) MARINATED IN LIME, TEQUILA, GARLIC & CHILIS.7.75

HOT PEPPER JACK QUESADILLA & SALSA TOMATILLO.........4.75

BAKED BRIE AND ROASTED GARLIC BULB..................5.75

GREEK FRITTATA OF ARTICHOKE HEARTS, FETA CHEESE, SPINACH, KALAMATA OLIVES & TOMATO.5.75

*EGGPLANT ROLLETINI STUFFED WITH RICOTTA, ASIAGO & BASIL IN SPICY TOMATO SAUCE...5.50

*CORN CHOWDER WITH BACON, RED POTATOES AND SUN DRIED TOMATOES...............4.25

EXECUTIVE CHEF: SUE WILKENS

SIDE ORDERS

ROASTED GARLIC BULB........75

ROASTED GARLIC BULB WITH IL FORNAIO BREAD & BUTTER..2.00

AIOLI OR SALSA TOMATILLO..75

BRUSCETTA: GRILLED PANE DEL FORNAIOBRUSHED WITH ROSEMARY-GARLIC OLIVE OIL........1.75

RED SKINNED POTATOES ROASTED WITH GARLIC-OLIVE OIL...1.75

POLENTA BAKED WITH ASIAGO AND SPICY TOMATO SAUCE......2.25

PASTA

BUCATINI WITH GRILLED TUSCANO AND/OR CALABRESE SAUSAGE AND SPICY TOMATO SAUCE......9.25

SPAGHETTI WITH WILD & DOMESTIC MUSHROOMS, ONION & BUTTER9.75

FETTUCCINE WITH GORGONZOLA-FORNAIOBRUSHED RED PEPPERCREAM SAUCE & TOASTED WALNUTS......10.00

LINGUINI WITH PRAWNS, PROS-CIUTTO AND GARLIC-CREAM SAUCE OR SPICY TOMATO SAUCE..10.75

*LINGUINI TUTTUMARE (MUSSELS, PRAWNS, CLAMS & MONKFISH IN TOMATO-RED WINE SAUCE)..10.50

*FETTUCCINE WITH CHICKEN, RED BELL PEPPERS, CUCUMBERS, PEAS & LEMON CREAM SAUCE.....10.00

ENTREES

*GRILLED CHICKEN BREAST PECAN CRUSTED WITH BOURBON SAUCE; LEMON RICE & ZUCCHINI..12.00

*BEEF BRAISED WITH RED WINE, DIJON MUSTARD & ROSEMARY; WITH PARSLEY BUTTERED EGG NOODLES & GREEN BEANS WITH CARROTS.13.00

*GRILLED WESTERN VEAL CHOP WITH ROASTED GARLIC BUTTER; WITH RED POTATO AND WILD MUSHROOM GRATIN & RED SWISS CHARD.15.00

*GRILLED BLACK TIP SHARK MAR-INATED IN TEQUILA, CHILIS & LIME; SERVED WITH OVEN ROAST POTATOES & GREEN BEANS..12.50

*BLUE NOSE SEA BASS IN PARCH-MENT WITH A GINGER-CILANTRO-LIME BUTTER; WITH LEMON RICE AND ZUCCHINI WITH BELL PEPPER AND CORN.............13.50

SALADS

MIXED SEASONAL GREENS WITH ANCHOVY-CAPER VINAIGRETTE4.25

PLUS TRIPLE-CREAM BLEU CHEESE & SEASONED WALNUTS......5.25

PLUS GRANA PADANO AND PINE NUTS......................5.25

SHREDDED ROMAINE AND SPINACH WITH PISTACHIOS, JICAMA, RED BELL PEPPERS & TOASTED CUMIN VINAIGRETTE.............4.75

WHOLE MILK MOZZARELLA AND ROASTED BELL PEPPERS WITH SUN DRIED TOMATO VINAIGRETTE5.50

SPINACH SALAD WITH BULGARIAN FETA CHEESE, KALAMATA OLIVES & RED ONION.........6.75

HALF SPINACH SALAD...5.25

*NICOISE SALAD WITH FRESHLY GRILLED MAHI MAHI, GREEN BEANS RED POTATOES, HARD-COOKED EGG & AIOLI.............8.75

*BLT SALAD WITH SHREDDED RO-MAINE, BACON, TOMATOES AND CREAMY BASIL DRESSING...5.50

LITTLE CITY

ANTIPASTI BAR

673 UNION ST.

SAN FRANCISCO

CALIFORNIA 94133

WHAT IS THE PROPER DISTANCE?

MASAAKI
OGAI

ILLUSTRATION

MASAAKI
OGAI

ILLUSTRATION

MASAAKI
OGAI

ILLUSTRATION

DESIGN FIRM: Dan Liew
Graphic Design,
San Francisco, California
DESIGNER: Dan Liew
ILLUSTRATOR: Masaaki
Ogai

MASAAKI
OGAI

ILLUSTRATION

TOM TRAPP
PRESIDENT

154 STAGE ROAD
MONROE
NEW YORK 10950
(914) 783-8424
FAX (914) 783-0830

DESIGN FIRM: Bear Brook

Design, Inc.,

Monroe, New York

ART DIRECTOR: Tom

Trapp

DESIGNER: JIm Hiller

154 STAGE ROAD
MONROE
NEW YORK 10950

Bear Brook Design, Inc.

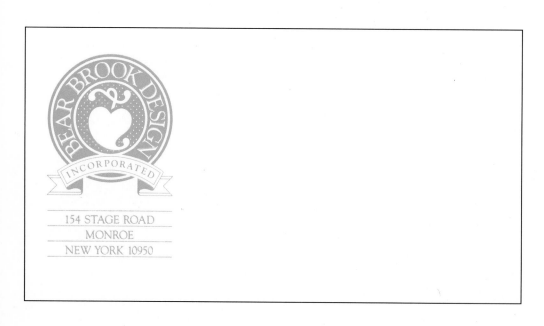

154 STAGE ROAD
MONROE
NEW YORK 10950

DESIGN FIRM: Vaughn/ Wedeen Creative, Albuquerque, New Mexico

DESIGNERS: Mark

Chamberlain, Steve Wedeen

ILLUSTRATOR: Mark Chamberlain

Convention Site: New Mexico Advertising Federation · P.O. Box 35972 · Albuquerque, New Mexico 87176 · (505) 881-0812
Coordinator: AAF Western Region Headquarters · 251 Post Street · San Francisco, California 94108 · (415) 421-6867

101

"Can you help me with my marketing problem?"

"Let me think about it a minute."

Art Bradshaw

Professional copywriter

2121 Felton St.

San Diego, CA. 92104

(619) 584-8747

Art Bradshaw
Professional copywriter

2121 Felton St.
San Diego, CA. 92104
(619) 584-8747

Art Bradshaw (Copywriter)

**DESIGN FIRM: Scott
Mayeda Art Direction
and Design, Del Mar,
California
ART DIRECTOR/
DESIGNER: Scott Mayeda**

"Let's get a martini, Art."

"Not tonight, I've got a job to do."

Hudson Hawk Films

DESIGN FIRM: Rod Dyer

Group, Inc.,

Los Angeles, California

DESIGNER: Rod Dyer

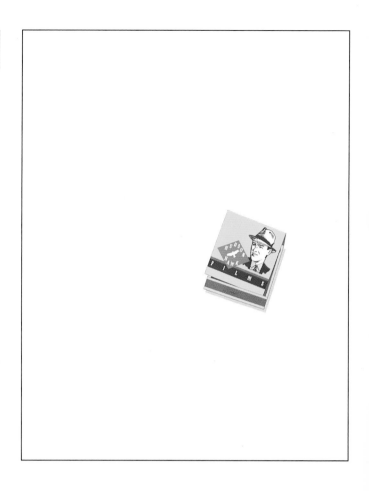

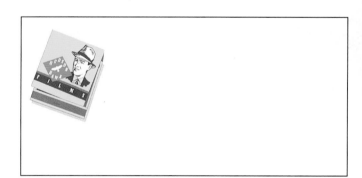

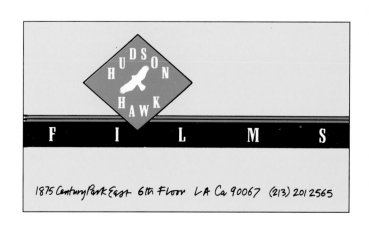

PUBLISHING INK.

521 State Street • Glendale, California 91203 • (818) 500-7857

DESIGN FIRM: Publishing

Ink, Glendale, California

CREATIVE DIRECTOR/

DESIGNER/ILLUSTRATOR:

Lisa Million Kent

Publishing Ink (Publishers of Computer Art)

ILLUSTRATION

31 Strong Place - apt. 3
Brooklyn, N.Y. 11231

7 1 8 . 7 9 7 . 0 3 4 8

Roxana Villa

ILLUSTRATION

31 Strong Place - apt. 3
Brooklyn, N.Y. 11231

7 1 8 . 7 9 7 . 0 3 4 8

INVOICE

DESIGN FIRM: Roxana

Villa Illustration,

Brooklyn, New York

DESIGNER/ILLUSTRATOR:

Roxana Villa

813/247-5508
P.O. Box 3245
Tampa, FL 33601-3245

DESIGN FIRM: Michael

Phillips Design,

Tampa, Florida

DESIGNER/ILLUSTRATOR:

Michael V. Phillips

Guavaween, Inc. (Tampa's Halloween Festival)

P.O. Box 3245
Tampa, FL 33601-3245

DESIGN FIRM: Anthony D'Agostino Design, Los Angeles, California

DESIGNER/ILLUSTRATOR: Anthony D'Agostino

Adrienne Weiss & Associates (Advertising and Design)

Warren Lynch & Associates, Inc.

1324 E. Washington Street
Louisville, Kentucky 40206
(502) 587-7722

Warren Lynch & Associates, Inc.

1324 E. Washington Street
Louisville, Kentucky 40206

DESIGN FIRM: Minnick
Advertising,
Louisville, Kentucky
DESIGNER: Norm Minnick
PHOTOGRAPHER: Warren
Lynch

Warren Lynch & Associates, Inc.

1324 E. Washington Street
Louisville, Kentucky 40206
(502) 587-7722

Warren Lynch & Associates, Inc.

1324 E. Washington Street
Louisville, Kentucky 40206
(502) 587-7722

Warren Lynch & Associates, Inc.

1324 E. Washington Street
Louisville, Kentucky 40206

109

DESIGNER/ILLUSTRATOR:

Melissa Grimes,

Austin, Texas

WATERBROOK WINERY

Waterbrook
Winery
Corporation

Route 1 Box 46
Lowden, WA 99360

DESIGN FIRM: Curtis

Design, Seattle,

Washington

DESIGNER/ILLUSTRATOR:

Laurie Curtis

WATERBROOK WINERY

Waterbrook
Winery
Corporation

Route 1 Box 46
Lowden, WA 99360

509 522-1918

Waterbrook Winery Corporation

THACHER & THOMPSON, ARCHITECTS
819½ PACIFIC AVE., SANTA CRUZ, CA 95060 (408) 426-4683

**DESIGN FIRM: Sue Crolick

Advertising & Design,

Minneapolis, Minnesota

DESIGNER: Sue Crolick

PHOTOGRAPHER: Kent

Severson

KEYLINER: Nancy Johnson

TYPOGRAPHY: Great

Faces**

Jean Flanagan (Seamstress/Dressmaker)

DESIGN FIRM: Robert

Flanagan Design,

San Jose, California

DESIGNER/ILLUSTRATOR:

Robert Flanagan

Jean Flanagan
Seamstress

1728 Myra Drive
San Jose, CA 95124
408.264.9648

David Albrecht Custom Tilesetting

DESIGN FIRM: Jim

Heimann Design,

Santa Monica, California

DESIGNER: Jim Heimann

DESIGNER/ILLUSTRATOR:

Lynn Schulte,

Minneapolis, Minnesota

DESIGN FIRM: Michael

Kennedy Associates,

Sacramento, California

DESIGNER: Michael

Kennedy

Michael Kennedy Associates (Design Firm)

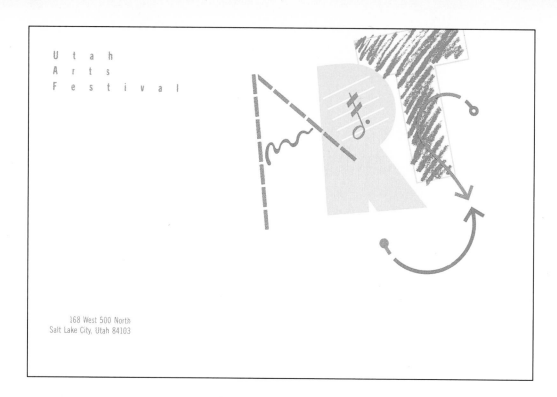

**DESIGN FIRM: LaPine/
O'Very, Salt Lake
City, Utah
DESIGNERS: Julia LaPine,
Traci O'Very Covey**

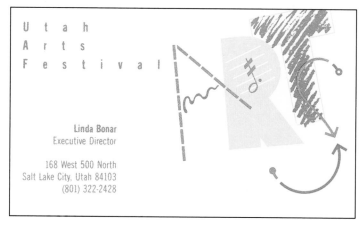

Linda Bonar
Executive Director

168 West 500 North
Salt Lake City, Utah 84103
(801) 322-2428

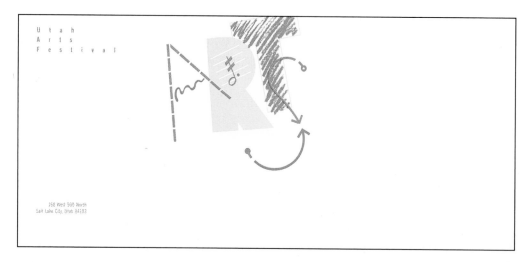

2 6 3 2 S. H A R B O R B L V D · **7 1 4 7 5 1 4 8 4 6** · S A N T A A N A C A 9 2 7 0 4

DESIGN FIRM: Hugh

Dunnahoe Illustration

& Design, Santa Ana,

California

DESIGNER/ILLUSTRATOR:

Hugh Dunnahoe

H	U	G	H
D	U N N A H O E		
I L L U S T R A T I O N			
&	D E S I G N		

2 6 3 2 S H A R B O R B L V D
S A N T A A N A C A 9 2 7 0 4

H	U	G	H
D	U N N A H O E		
I L L U S T R A T I O N			
&	D E S I G N		

2 6 3 2 S. H A R B O R B L V D · **7 I 4 7 5 I 4 8 4 6** · S A N T A A N A C A 9 2 7 0 4

INVOICE

DATE

JOB
DESCRIPTION

TAX

TOTAL

TERMS

Any unpaid balance from this invoice after 30 days will accrue a 1½% per month interest charge until paid.
Should it become necessary to legally enforce the provisions of this invoice, the purchaser agrees to pay reasonable attorney and/or collection agency fees and costs.

The Wendy Weil Agency, Inc.
747 Third Avenue
New York, New York 10017

Telephone: 212-753-2605

Cable: TURTLES NEW YORK
Telex: 668 359
Fax: 212-688-8297

DESIGNER: Michael

Trossman, New York,

New York

PHOTOGRAPHER: E.J.

Carr

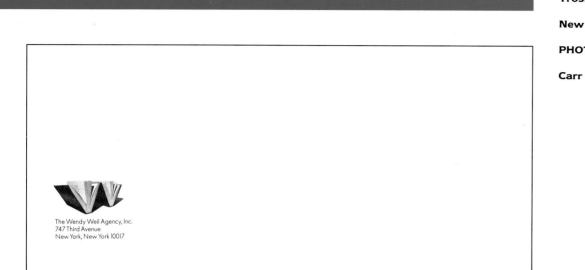

The Wendy Weil Agency, Inc.
747 Third Avenue
New York, New York 10017

The Wendy Weil Agency, Inc.
747 Third Avenue
New York, New York 10017

212-753-2605

Cable: TURTLES NEW YORK
Telex: 668 359

The Wendy Weil Agency, Inc.
747 Third Avenue
New York, New York 10017

DESIGN FIRM: Lauren

Smith Design,

Palo Alto, California

DESIGNER/ILLUSTRATOR:

Lauren Smith

ADVERTISING AFTER HOURS 944 COWPER STREET, PALO ALTO, CALIFORNIA 94301, (415) 325-2827

BUSINESS HOURS: 5PM TO 8AM

DESIGN FIRM: Lauren

Smith Design,

Palo Alto, California

ART DIRECTOR/

ILLUSTRATOR: Lauren

Smith

DESIGNERS: Lauren

Smith, Donna Lang

W   E   A   V   E   R

Weaver Photography
291 Tyrella Avenue
Mountain View, CA 94043
(415) 961-8731

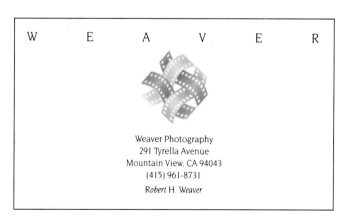

W   E   A   V   E   R

Weaver Photography
291 Tyrella Avenue
Mountain View, CA 94043
(415) 961-8731
Robert H. Weaver

Bob Weaver Photography

Fine Print, Ltd., 4657 N. Ravenswood, Chicago, IL 60640

Telephone 312/334-4382

TYPOGRAPHERS

DESIGN FIRM: William

Hafeman Design,

Chicago, Illinois

DESIGNER: William

Hafeman

ILLUSTRATORS: Christi

Rager, Eric Tryba

2M Sets. 3-85. Nu-Tone Printing Company. 352-1000

Fine Print, Ltd., 4657 N. Ravenswood, Chicago, IL 60640

Telephone 312/334-4382

To:

Date

INVOICE

Job Description

Quantity

Amount

T Y P O G R A P H E R S

Fine Print, Ltd., 4657 N. Ravenswood, Chicago, IL 60640

T Y P O G R A P H E R S

DESIGN FIRM: Rauchman Rauchman & Associates, **DESIGNERS:** Bob Miami, Florida Rauchman, Mindy Vernon **ART DIRECTOR:** Bob

COCONUT GROVE ASSOCIATION, INC./SPONSOR OF THE COCONUT GROVE ARTS FESTIVAL
Suite 302, 2701 South Bayshore Drive, Coconut Grove, Florida 33133. (305) 858-2950

LYCEUM

Fellowship

1000 Massachusetts Avenue   Cambridge, Massachusetts 02138

LYCEUM

Fellowship

1000 Massachusetts Avenue   Cambridge, Massachusetts 02138

(6 1 7)   5 4 7 - 5 4 0 0

A society sponsoring

lecture series open to

the community.

DESIGN FIRM: Skolos

Wedell + Raynor

Inc., Charlestown,

Massachusetts

DESIGNER: Cheryl Lilley

Shea

Lyceum Fellowship Committee

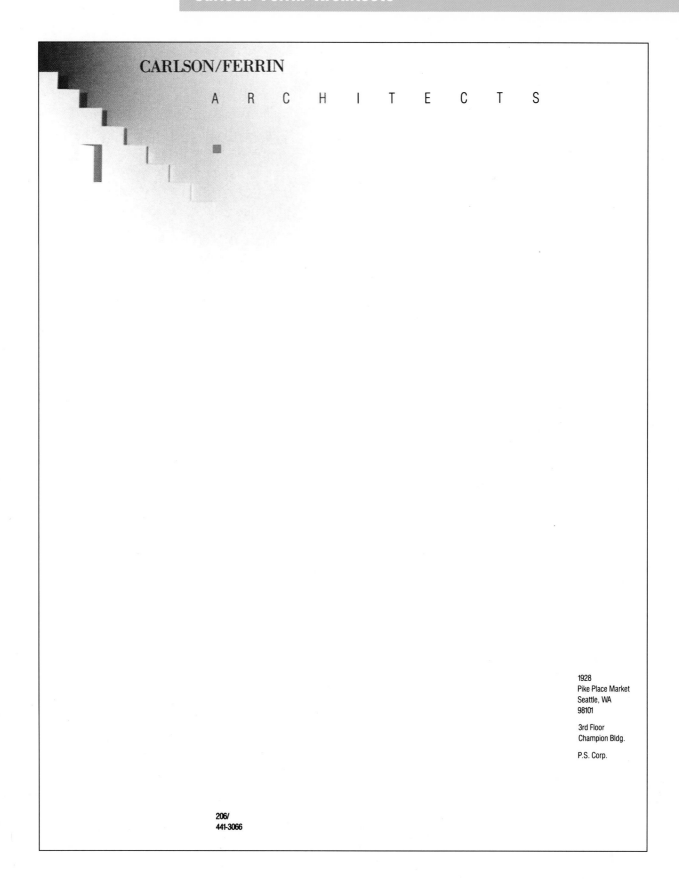

CARLSON/FERRIN

A R C H I T E C T S

1928
Pike Place Market
Seattle, WA
98101

3rd Floor
Champion Bldg.

P.S. Corp.

206/
441-3066

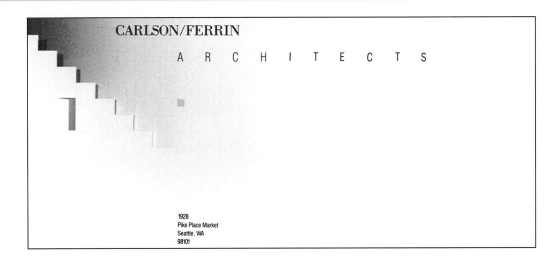

DESIGN FIRM: Hornall
Anderson Design
Works, Seattle,
Washington
ART DIRECTOR/
DESIGNER: Jack Anderson
PHOTOGRAPHER: Greg
Krogstad

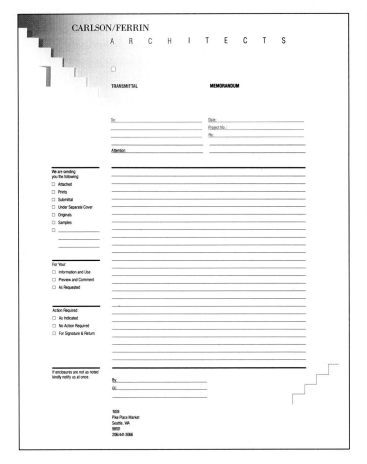

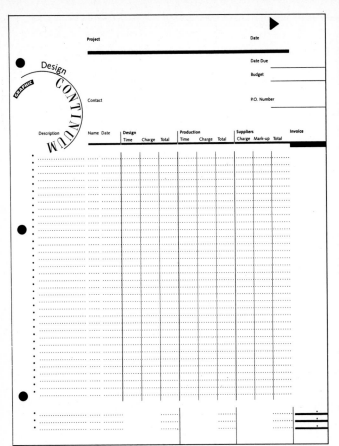

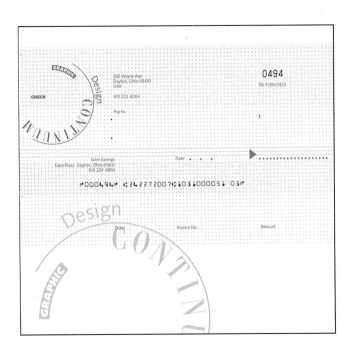

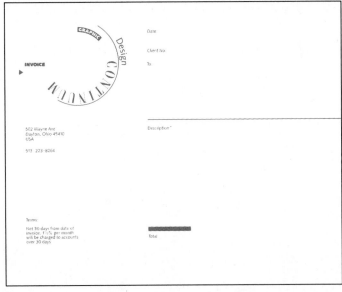

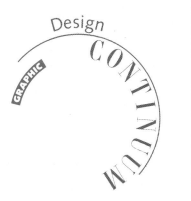

DESIGN FIRM: Graphic

Design Continuum,

Dayton, Ohio

DESIGNERS: John Emery,

Dwayne Swormstedt

513 223·8264

502 Wayne Ave.
Dayton, Ohio 45410
USA

502 Wayne Ave.
Dayton, Ohio 45410

USA

WASHBURN
CHILD
GUIDANCE
CENTER

2 • 4 • 3 • 0
NICOLLET
AVENUE
SOUTH

MINNEAPOLIS
MINNESOTA
5 5 . 4 0 4
612•871•1454

DESIGN FIRM: Duffy
Design Group,
Minneapolis, Minnesota
DESIGNER/ILLUSTRATOR:
Charles Spencer
Anderson

Dear Washburn Center
Before I came to Washburn
I couldn't read good. I got
mad lot of time. It was
real hard to go to school.
The washburn teachers are
nice ladys and the man.
I learn to stop and think
befor I get mad. I can
count good and read good.
I make new friends I
don't feel like old Joseph
anymore. I'm a new Joseph.
I like myself

        Joseph

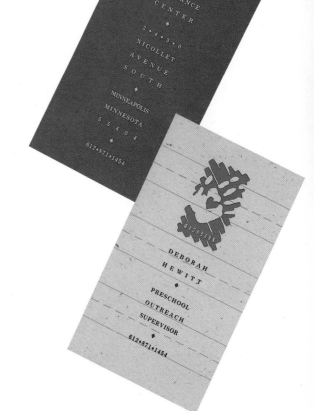

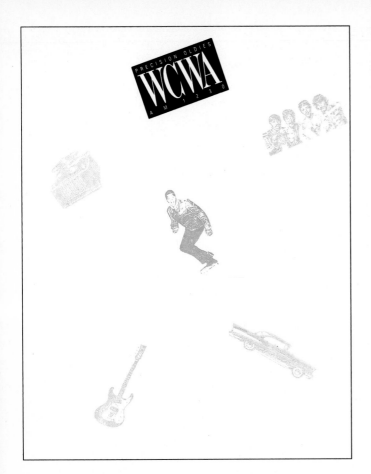

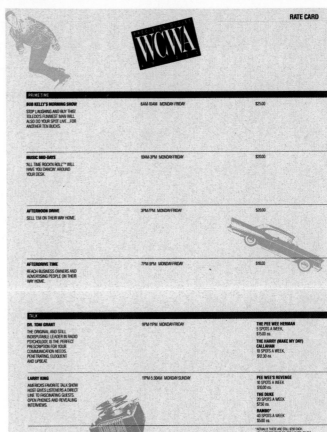

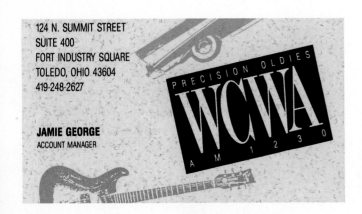

124 N. SUMMIT STREET
SUITE 400
FORT INDUSTRY SQUARE
TOLEDO, OHIO 43604
419-248-2627

JAMIE GEORGE
ACCOUNT MANAGER

DESIGN FIRM: Lesniewicz/

Navarre,

Toledo, Ohio

DESIGNER: Terry

Lesniewicz

WCWA AM 1230

124 N. SUMMIT STREET
SUITE 400
FORT INDUSTRY SQUARE
TOLEDO, OHIO 43604
419-248-2627

DESIGN FIRM: Janis

Boehm Design,

Chicago, Illinois

DESIGNERS: Janis Boehm,

Tracy Gibbons

JANIS
BOEHM
DESIGN

JANIS BOEHM
PRINCIPAL

345 NORTH CANAL STREET
CHICAGO, ILLINOIS 60606
312.993.0405

JANIS
BOEHM
DESIGN

JANIS BOEHM
PRINCIPAL

345 NORTH CANAL STREET
CHICAGO, ILLINOIS 60606
312.993.0405

JANIS
BOEHM
DESIGN

JANIS BOEHM
PRINCIPAL

345 NORTH CANAL STREET
CHICAGO, ILLINOIS 60606
312.993.0405

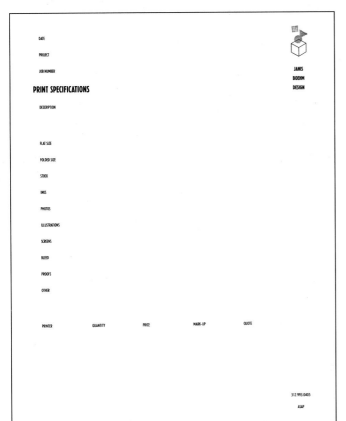

DATE

PROJECT

JOB NUMBER

PRINT SPECIFICATIONS

DESCRIPTION

FLAT SIZE

FOLDED SIZE

STOCK

INKS

PHOTOS

ILLUSTRATIONS

SCREENS

BLEED

PROOFS

OTHER

PRINTER   QUANTITY   PRICE   MARK-UP   QUOTE

JANIS
BOEHM
DESIGN

312.993.0405

ASAP

JANIS
BOEHM
DESIGN

345
NORTH
CANAL
STREET
CHICAGO
ILLINOIS
60606

DESIGN FIRM: Eberle

Design, Venice,

California

ART DIRECTOR/

DESIGNER: Linda Eberle

Gayda-Hoptman Photography

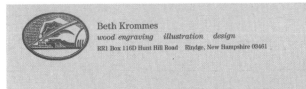

Beth Krommes

wood engraving   illustration   design

RR1 Box 116D Hunt Hill Road   Rindge, New Hampshire 03461

DESIGNER/ILLUSTRATOR:

Beth Krommes,

Rindge, New Hampshire

Beth Krommes

*wood engraving
illustration
design*

RR1 Box 116D
Hunt Hill Road
Rindge
New Hampshire
03461
(603) 899-6061

Beth Krommes

*wood engraving
illustration
design*

RR1 Box 116D, Hunt Hill Road
Rindge, New Hampshire 03461
(603) 899-6061

Beth Krommes (Wood Engraving, Illustration and Design)

P.O. BOX 1703
BATON ROUGE
LOUISIANA 70821
504 383 3880

DESIGN FIRM: Charlie

Th'ng Design,

Baton Rouge, Louisiana

DESIGNER: Charlie Th'ng

DAVID HUMPHREYS
PHOTOGRAPHER

P.O. BOX 1703
BATON ROUGE
LOUISIANA 70821
504 383 3880

David Humphreys Photography

Robin Bugbee (Personal Stationery)

DESIGN FIRM: Pirtle Design, Dallas, Texas

DESIGNER/ILLUSTRATOR: Woody Pirtle

R O B I N   B U G B E E

DESIGN FIRM: LaPine/
O'Very, Salt Lake
City, Utah
DESIGNER/ILLUSTRATOR:
Julia LaPine

SKY, FOLIAGE, SOIL
BLOOM HEDGES
SUNLIGHT, AIR
WATER, DETAIL
VINE, FRAGRANCE
STYLE DESIGN
JONATHAN R. BELL
RESIDENTIAL
LANDSCAPE
ARCHITECTURE
730 JUDSON AVE.
HIGHLAND PARK
ILLINOIS 60035
312-432-7525 ASLA

SKY, FOLIAGE, SOIL
BLOOM HEDGES
SUNLIGHT, AIR
WATER, DETAIL
VINE, FRAGRANCE
STYLE DESIGN
JONATHAN R. BELL
RESIDENTIAL
LANDSCAPE
ARCHITECTURE
730 JUDSON AVE.
HIGHLAND PARK
ILLINOIS 60035
312-432-7525 ASLA

DESIGN FIRM: Hornall Anderson Design Works, Seattle, Washington

ART DIRECTOR: John Hornall

DESIGNERS: Juliet Shen, Julie Tanagi

ILLUSTRATOR: Mark Grabow

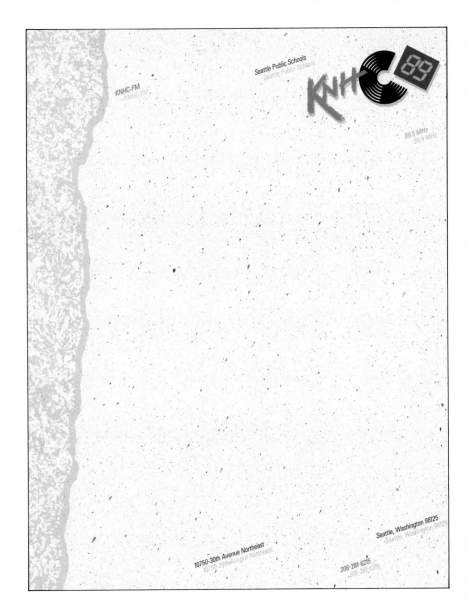

KNHC 89 FM

Peter Steiner Photography

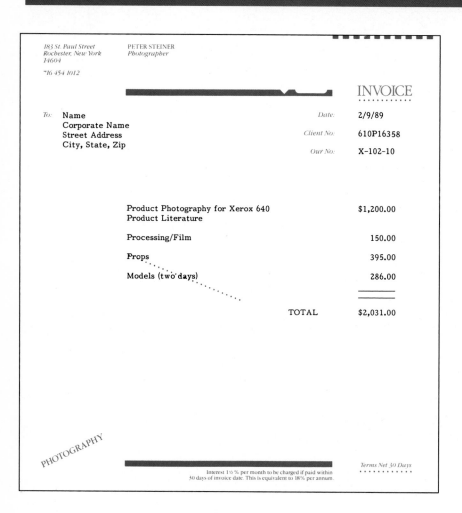

183 St. Paul Street
Rochester, New York
14604

716 454 1012

PETER STEINER
Photographer

INVOICE

To: Name
Corporate Name
Street Address
City, State, Zip

Date: 2/9/89

Client No: 610P16358

Our No: X-102-10

Product Photography for Xerox 640 Product Literature	$1,200.00
Processing/Film	150.00
Props	395.00
Models (two days)	286.00
TOTAL	$2,031.00

PHOTOGRAPHY

Terms Net 30 Days

Interest 1½ % per month to be charged if paid within
30 days of invoice date. This is equivalent to 18% per annum.

DESIGN FIRM: James L.

Selak Design,

Fairport, New York

ART DIRECTOR/

DESIGNER: James L. Selak

TYPOGRAPHY: Total

Typography

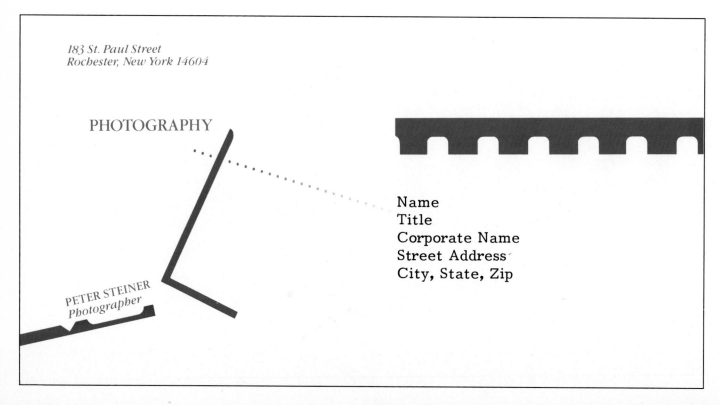

183 St. Paul Street
Rochester, New York 14604

PHOTOGRAPHY

PETER STEINER
Photographer

Name
Title
Corporate Name
Street Address
City, State, Zip

183 St. Paul Street
Rochester, New York 14604

PETER STEINER
Photographer
Represented by
GRACE A. LAWLOR

716 454 1012

February 9, 1989

Name
Title
Corporate Name
Street Address
City, State, Zip

Dear Sirs:

When the typewritten message is added to a letterhead, it should
have a balancing effect on the design elements of that letterhead.
So, it's actually the secretary who completes the letterhead design
with her typing format.

I believe that the contemporary format shown here contributes to
the visual balance of the page and thus enhances the new design;
paragraphs are not to be indented in this format.

As this sheet demonstrates, the secretary should always start
the correspondence with the position dot which will ensure that
a consistant and unified visual statement is made every time.

Very Cordially,

James L. Selak
Title

JLS/v

PHOTOGRAPHY

DESIGN FIRM: Duffy

Design Group,

Minneapolis,

Minnesota

DESIGNER: Charles

Spencer Anderson

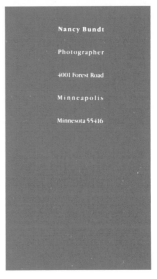

DAVID
HARRELL   ADVERTISING   57½   ATLANTA   404
          COPY &   THIRTEENTH   GEORGIA   876 0719
          CREATIVE   STREET   30309
          DIRECTION

ART DIRECTOR/CREATIVE

DIRECTOR:

David Harrell, Atlanta,

Georgia

DESIGNER: Nancy Neal

Hughes

ILLUSTRATOR: Rose

Whitaker

DAVID   ADVERTISING   57½   ATLANTA   404
HARRELL   COPY &   THIRTEENTH   GEORGIA   876 0719
             CREATIVE   STREET   30309
             DIRECTION

DAVID HARRELL   ADVERTISING COPY & CREATIVE DIRECTION   57½ THIRTEENTH STREET   ATLANTA GEORGIA 30309

DAVID HARRELL   ADVERTISING COPY & CREATIVE DIRECTION   57½ THIRTEENTH STREET   ATLANTA GEORGIA 30309   404 876 0719

INVOICE

TO

DATE

OUR JOB NO.

INVOICE NO.

FOR

THE FULL AMOUNT OF THIS INVOICE IS
DUE WITHIN 30 DAYS. A CHARGE OF 1½%
PER MONTH MAY BE ADDED TO ANY
AMOUNT 30 DAYS OR MORE IN ARREARS.
THANK YOU FOR YOUR PAYMENT.

TOTAL DUE

David Harrell (Copywriter & Creative Director)

DESIGN FIRM: Lowell

Williams Design,

Inc., Houston, Texas

ART DIRECTOR/

DESIGNER: Lowell

Williams

ILLUSTRATOR: Lisa

Dolginoff

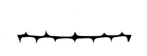

MARILYN THOMPSON
CHAIRSIDE ASSISTANT

DAVID LEE FULENWIDER, D. D. S.
FAMILY DENTISTRY

UNIVERSITY MEDICAL CENTER
5620 GREENBRIAR, SUITE 101
HOUSTON, TEXAS 77005
(713) 524-9373

DAVID LEE FULENWIDER, D. D. S.
FAMILY DENTISTRY

UNIVERSITY MEDICAL CENTER
5620 GREENBRIAR, SUITE 101
HOUSTON, TEXAS 77005
(713) 524-9373

DAVID LEE FULENWIDER, D. D. S.
FAMILY DENTISTRY

UNIVERSITY MEDICAL CENTER
5620 GREENBRIAR, SUITE 101
HOUSTON, TEXAS 77005
(713) 524-9373

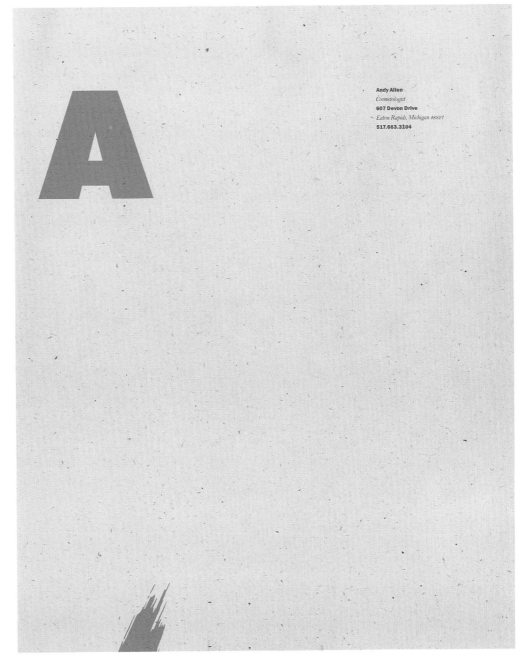

DESIGN FIRM: Tim Hartford Graphic Design, Chicago, Illinois

ART DIRECTOR/ DESIGNER/ CALLIGRAPHER: Tim Hartford

TYPOGRAPHY: The Typesmiths

DESIGN FIRM: Pont Street,

Seattle,

Washington

DESIGNER: Greg Carr

DESIGN FIRM: Rauchman

& Associates,

Miami, Florida

ART DIRECTOR: Bob

Rauchman

DESIGNERS: Bob

Rauchman, Mindy

Vernon

Halpern Construction Company. 3129 North 29 Avenue, Hollywood, Florida 33020.   Dade: 754-0588.   Broward: 921-0588.

Halpern Construction Company. 3129 North 29 Avenue, Hollywood, Florida 33020.

Kent R. Brown, D.D.S.
Family Dentistry
4805 River Oaks Blvd.
Fort Worth, Texas 76114
(817) 625-1548

Kent R. Brown, D.D.S.

DESIGN FIRM: Main

Station Unlimited,

Fort Worth, Texas

DESIGNER: Bob Walter

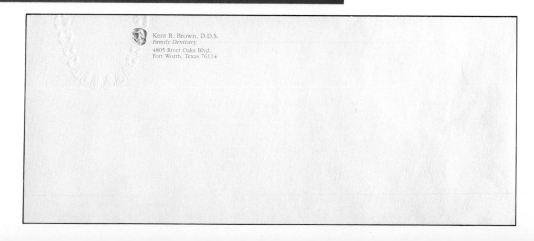

Kent R. Brown, D.D.S.
Family Dentistry
4805 River Oaks Blvd.
Fort Worth, Texas 76114

G J PHILLIPS DDS

ORTHODONTICS FOR

ADULTS · CHILDREN

1212 E JOPPA ROAD

TOWSON MD 21204

301 · 825 · 1771

G J PHILLIPS DDS

ORTHODONTICS FOR

ADULTS · CHILDREN

1212 E JOPPA ROAD

TOWSON MD 21204

DESIGN FIRM: David

Ashton and Company,

Baltimore, Maryland

DESIGNER/ILLUSTRATOR:

Jennifer Phillips

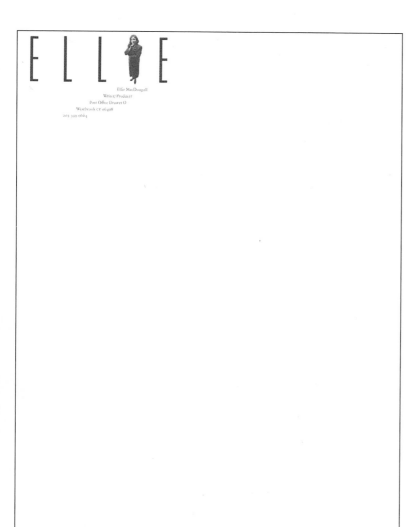

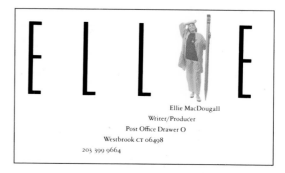

DESIGN FIRM: Appleton Design, Hartford, Connecticut

ART DIRECTOR: Robert Appleton

DESIGNERS: Robert Appleton, Christopher Passehl

PHOTOGRAPHER: Frank Marchese

TYPOGRAPHY: New England Typographic Service

Gina Stephenson

Mark J. Perelmuter, D.M.D., M.S.
Orthodontist

1112 Dupont Circle
Louisville, KY 40207
502 897-1112

8005 Postal Way
Okolona, KY 40219
502 969-4111

Mark J. Perelmuter, D.M.D., M.S.
Orthodontist

1112 Dupont Circle
Louisville, KY 40207
502 897-1112

8005 Postal Way
Okolona, KY 40219
502 969-4111

Mark J. Perelmuter, D.M.D., M.S.
Orthodontist

DESIGN FIRM: Images,

Louisville,

Kentucky

ART DIRECTOR: Julius

Friedman

DESIGNER: Carol

Eberhardt

Mark J. Perelmuter Orthodontist

The American Society for the Prevention of Cruelty to Animals
441 East 92nd St · New York, NY 10128 · 212·876·7000

A. S. P. C. A.

The American Society for the Prevention of Cruelty to Animals · 441 East 92nd St · New York, NY 10128 · 212·876·7000

GILBERT® oxford Bond, White, 24 lb.

A student-designed

letterhead for

a Gilbert Paper promotion.

DESIGN FIRM: Yelton/

Kennerly, Inc.,

Appleton, Wisconsin

ART DIRECTOR: Jeffrey

Yelton

DESIGNER: Susan Stern

Association for the Prevention of Cruelty to Animals

A. S. P. C. A.

The American Society for the Prevention of Cruelty to Animals · 441 East 92nd St. · New York, NY 10128 · 212·876·7000

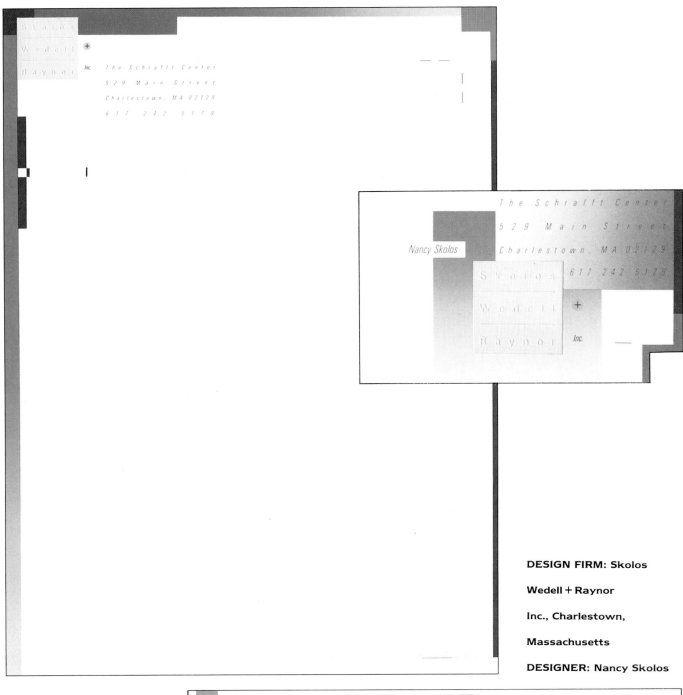

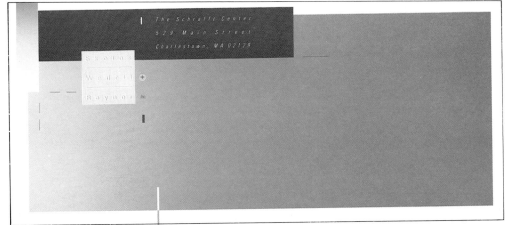

DESIGN FIRM: Skolos

Wedell + Raynor

Inc., Charlestown,

Massachusetts

DESIGNER: Nancy Skolos

R.R. 2 Box 38
Greencastle, Indiana 46135
317 · 653 · 9500

DESIGN & ART PRODUCTION
R.R. 2 Box 38
Greencastle, Indiana 46135
317 · 653 · 9500

R.R. 2 Box 38
Greencastle, Indiana 46135

J·A·N·A·E

B·E·R·R·Y

P U R C H A S E O R D E R	
TO	DATE
	P.O. NUMBER
	ORDERED BY
	CLIENT/ JOB NUMBER

JOB DESCRIPTION

ESTIMATED COST	DELIVERY DATE

R.R. 2 Box 38
Greencastle, Indiana 46135
317 · 653 · 9500

DESIGNER: Janae Berry,

Greencastle, Indiana

ILLUSTRATOR: Bruce Dean

TYPOGRAPHY: Hunt Type

J·A·N·A·E

B·E·R·R·Y

R.R. 2 Box 38
Greencastle, Indiana 46135

SANDI PIERANTOZZI
GRAPHIC DESIGN
1532 SANSOM STREET
PHILADELPHIA
PENNSYLVANIA
19102
215/751-9093

DESIGN FIRM: Sandi
Pierantozzi Graphic
Design, Philadelphia,
Pennsylvania
DESIGNER: Sandi
Pierantozzi

SANDI PIERANTOZZI
GRAPHIC DESIGN
1532 SANSOM STREET
PHILADELPHIA
PENNSYLVANIA
19102
215/751-9093

SANDI PIERANTOZZI
GRAPHIC DESIGN
1532 SANSOM STREET
PHILADELPHIA
PENNSYLVANIA
19102

Sandi Pierantozzi Graphic Design

13 Phillips Street/South Natick, Mass. 01760
Telephone/617-653-7404

13 Phillips Street/South Natick, Massachusetts 01760/617-653-7404

13 Phillips Street
South Natick, Mass.
01760

DESIGNER/ILLUSTRATOR:

Gael Burns,

South Natick,

Massachusetts

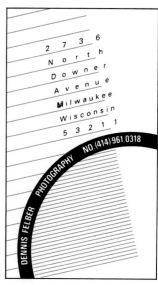

DESIGNER: Greg Montezon, Chicago, Illinois

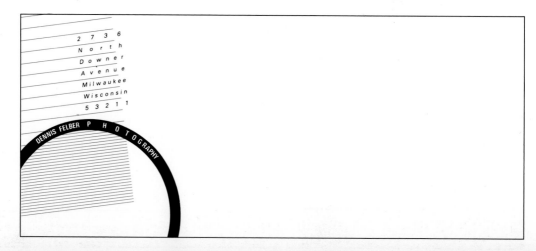

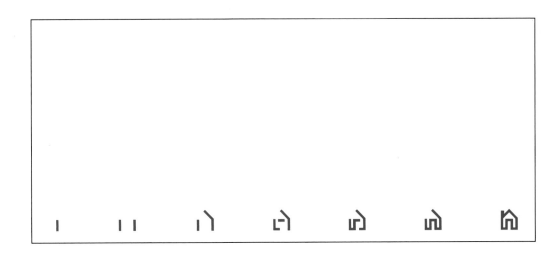

Michelle Belden A.I.A.
Architect

125 University Avenue
Palo Alto, California 94301
(415) 321-9677

DESIGN FIRM: Gagarin

McGeoch, Palo

Alto, California

ART DIRECTOR/

DESIGNER: Mark McGeoch

Michelle Belden, A.I.A. (Architect)

ROWDY CREATIVE, INC. 417 Union Plaza • 333 N. Washington Ave. • Mpls., MN 55401 • (612) 349-2702

ROWDY CREATIVE, INC.
409 Union Plaza • 333 N. Washington Ave.
Mpls., MN 55401 • (612) 349-2702

DESIGN FIRM: Rowdy

Creative, Inc.,

Minneapolis, Minnesota

DESIGNERS: Chuck Batko,

Paul Hagen

ROWDY CREATIVE, INC.
417 Union Plaza • 333 N. Washington Ave • Mpls., MN 55401

Paul R. Hagen

(612) 349-2702

SANDRA HEINEN, INC.
ARTISTS REPRESENTATIVE

1913 EWING AVENUE SO.
MINNEAPOLIS
MINNESOTA 55416
(612) 332-3671

Sandra Heinen (Artists' Representative)

SANDRA HEINEN, INC.
ARTISTS REPRESENTATIVE
1913 EWING AVENUE SO.
MINNEAPOLIS
MINNESOTA 55416
(612) 332-3671

DESIGN FIRM: Sue Crolick

Advertising

& Design, Minneapolis,

Minnesota

DESIGNER: Sue Crolick

PHOTOGRAPHER: Mark

La Favor

RETOUCHER: Gordon

Thorstad

KEYLINER: Nancy Johnson

TYPOGRAPHY: Great

Faces

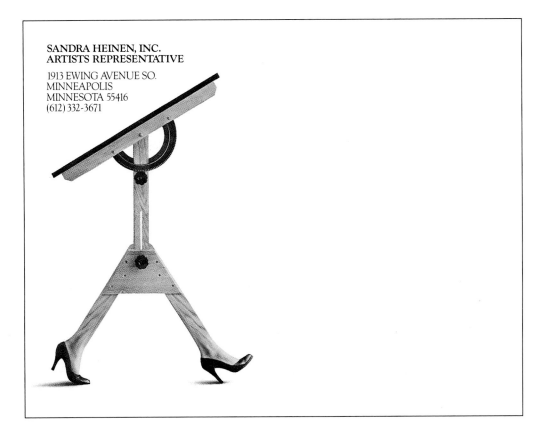

SANDRA HEINEN, INC.
ARTISTS REPRESENTATIVE

1913 EWING AVENUE SO.
MINNEAPOLIS
MINNESOTA 55416
(612) 332-3671

SANDRA HEINEN, INC.
ARTISTS REPRESENTATIVE
1913 EWING AVENUE SO.
MINNEAPOLIS
MINNESOTA 55416
(612) 332-3671

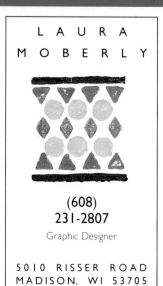

L A U R A
M O B E R L Y

(608)
231-2807

Graphic Designer

5010 RISSER ROAD
MADISON, WI 53705

DESIGNER: Laura

Moberly, Madison,

Wisconsin

L A U R A   M O B E R L Y

5010 RISSER ROAD   MADISON, WI 53705
6 0 8 • 2 3 1 • 2 8 0 7

DESIGN FIRM: Studio

Supplee, Houston,

Texas

ART DIRECTOR/

DESIGNER: Bonnie

Supplee

ILLUSTRATOR: Becky

O'Bryan Prejean

730 EAST 10TH STREET
HOUSTON, TEXAS 77008

730 EAST 10TH STREET
HOUSTON, TEXAS 77008
(713) 862-1543

Heger Photography

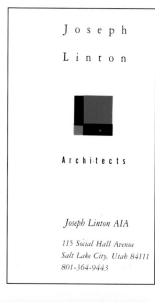

Joseph

Linton

Architects

Joseph Linton AIA

115 Social Hall Avenue
Salt Lake City, Utah 84111
801-364-9443

DESIGN FIRM: Raymond

Morales Design,

Highland, Utah

DESIGNER/ILLUSTRATOR:

Raymond Morales

Joseph Linton Architects

J   o   s   e   p   h

Architects

115 Social Hall Avenue
Salt Lake City, Utah 84111
801-364-9443

L   i   n   t   o   n

DESIGNER/ILLUSTRATOR:

Mary Leather,

Neptune, New Jersey

DESIGN FIRM: Morla

Design, San

Francisco, California

DESIGNER: Jennifer Morla

Precision Painters

CLIENTS

Advertising After Hours 122
Albrecht, David, Custom Tilesetting 114
Allen, Andrew 151
American Advertising Federation 101
American Institute of Architects 71
Archetype Architecture 29
Arizona Portfolio 25
Art Directors Club of Boston 38
Association for the Prevention of Cruelty to Animals 158
Bair, Ted, of Robert Glenn Design 115
Barnhart, Teddie 14
Bean, Brad, Photography 55
Bear Brook Design 100
Belden, Michelle, A.I.A. 165
Bell, Jonathan R., Landscape Architect 142
Bergen, Richard, Photography 36
Berry, Janae 60
Blue, Janice, Photo Stylist 70
Boehm, Janis, Design 136
Boguch, Sharon 81
Bradshaw, Art 102
Brown, Kent R., D.D.S. 154
Buck, Gary C. 50
Bugbee, Robin 141
Bundt, Nancy, Photography 146
Burns, Gael 163
Carlson Ferrin Architects 128
Carter, William E., Construction 93
Coconut Grove Association 126
Columbia Albums 86
Commercial Lithographing 78
Common Threads 87
Cooper, JoAnne 30
DeNeve, Rose 60
Dough Art 37
Dunnahoe, Hugh, Illustration 118

Fabulous Fifties Café 20
Felber, Dennis, Photography 164
Fine Print Ltd. Typographers 124
Fire Suppression Technologies 62
Flanagan, Jean 114
Foodesign 32
Fox, B.D., & Friends 47
Fulenwider, David Lee, D.D.S. 150
Gayda-Hoptman Photography 138
Giannetti Photography 72
Gladych, Marianne, Design 74
Goebel Photography 26
Gonzalez, Domingo, Design 90
Graphic Design Continuum 130
Graphic Solutions 42
Grimes, Melissa 110
Grossman, Myron, Illustration 16
Guavaween, Inc. 106
Halpern Construction 153
Harrell, David 148
Heger Photography 171
Heinen, Sandra 168
Hudson Hawk Films 103
Humphreys, David, Photography 140
Institute for the Study of Professional Risk 88
IVAC Corp. 82
Jacomini & Duda Design & Illustration 68
Java City 22
Jenkins, Jo Ann 152
Kelly, Kevin P., Realty &

Mortgage 80
Kennedy, Michael, Associates 115
KNHC 89 FM 143
Krommes, Beth 139
Lemon Grass Restaurant 63
Lieser, Ron, Design 92
Liller, Tamara, Photography 7
Linton, Joseph, Architects 172
Little City Restaurant 96
Lodestar Productions 56
Lots of Autos 23
Love, Mildred, A.I.A. 28
Lyceum Fellowship Committee 127
Lyles, Lizabeth Kelly 17
Lynch, Warren, Photography 108
MacDougall, Ellie 156
Medical Innovation Capital, Inc. 48
Melons Gift Shop 173
Moberly, Laura 170
Monighan + Terry, Architects 6
MusiCum Laude 41
Native American Art 94
Neat Seats 37
Ogai, Masaaki, Illustration 98
Peek, Lori Adamski 54
Perelmuter, Mark J., Orthodontist 157
Phillips, G.J., D.D.S. 155
Pierantozzi, Sandi, Graphic Design 162
Precision Painters 173
Publishing Ink 104
Real Art Ways 39
Riley Hospital for Children 46
Roberts, Scott, Architectural Illustration 58
Rowdy Creative 166
Salisbury, Mike, Communications 84
Sands, Richard, Productions 76

Shepherd, Robin, Studios 18
Skolos Wedell + Raynor 159
Slothower, Andrew, Design 44
Steiner, Peter, Photography 144
Sunflor 61
Texas Hotel 36
Thacher & Thompson 113
Tumbles, J.W. 64
Tumbleweed Restaurant 66
U.S. Mayors Conference 11
Utah Arts Festival 116
Villa, Roxana, Illustration 105
Walker, Ann, Catering 33
Walton, Brenda, Calligraphy & Illustration 12
Washburn Child Guidance Center 132
Waterbrook Winery Corp. 112
WCWA AM 1230 134
Weaver, Bob, Photography 123
Weil, Wendy, Agency, The 120
Weiss, Adrienne, & Associates 107
Weitz, Karen, Productions 40
Wings Fashion Apparel 95
Wolk, Michael, Design 24
Woolsey, David T., Landscape Architect 52
Zangrilli, Cathy 77
Zemke, Deborah, Illustration 8
Zimbler, Seymour, M.D. 34
Zumbo, Matt, Illustration 10

DESIGN FIRMS

Appleton Design 39, 156
Ashton, David, & Co. 155
Bear Brook Design 100
Blik, Tyler A., Design 28
Boehm, Janis, Design 136
Brock, Michael, Design 66
CBS Records 86
Cole & Weber 11
Collins Design Group 38
Conte, Christina, Advertising/ Design 32
Cook & Shanosky Associates 60
CooperWingard Design 30
Crolick, Sue, Advertising & Design 72, 113, 168
Curtis Design 112
D'Agostino, Anthony, Design 107
Darnell Design 37
Davis, Nancy, Design 86
DeFino, Perry, Graphic Design 90
Design Solutions 46
Duffy Design Group, The 48, 132, 146
Dunlavey Studio, The 6, 20, 22, 63
Dunnahoe, Hugh, Illustration 118
Dyer, Rod, Group, Inc. 103
Eberle Design 138
Fisher Design 80
Flanagan, Robert, Design 114
Fox, B.D., & Friends, Inc. 47

Gagarin McGeoch 164
Gagnon, W. Joseph, Design 81
Gardner's Graphic Hands 26
Gladych, Marianne, Design 74
Graphic Design Continuum 130
Graphic Solutions 42
Grossman, Myron, Illustration 16
Hafeman, William, Design 124
Hartford, Tim, Graphic Design 151
Heimann, Jim, Design 114
Hornall Anderson Design Works 128, 143
Hubbard & Hubbard Design 25
Images 157
Independent Project Press 36
Jacomini & Duda Design & Illustration 68
Kennedy, Michael, Associates 93, 115
Kilmer, Kira, Design 58
LaPine/O'Very 116, 142
Lesniewicz/Navarre 134
Lieser, Ron, Design 92
Liew, Dan, Graphic Design 98
Lodestar Productions 56
Loucks Atelier, Inc. 70
Main Station Unlimited 154
Mayeda, Scott, Art Direction & Design 102
Minnick Advertising 108
Mires Design, Inc. 82
Morales, Raymond, Design 172
Morla Design 173
Napoles & Associates 33
Obata-Kuechner, Inc. 37
Phillips, Michael, Design 106
Pierantozzi, Sandi, Graphic Design 162
Pirtle Design 141
Pont Street 152
PriceWeber Marketing Communications 78
Publishing Ink 104
Rauchman & Associates 126, 153
Richardson or Richardson 64

Rowdy Creative 166
Rubin Cordaro Design 71
Salisbury, Mike, Communications 84
Seifer, Barry, & Co. 88
Selak, James L., Design 144
Shalit, Eric, Designs 61
Shepherd, Robin, Studios 18, 94, 95
Skolos Wedell + Raynor 29, 127, 159
Slothower, Andrew, Design 44
Smith, Lauren, Design 122, 123
Studio Supplee 170
Sturdivant, Ray, Graphic Design 23
Taflan, Peter, Marketing Communications 62
Thiel Visual Design 10
Th'ng, Charlie, Design 140
Vaughn/Wedeen Creative 101
Villa, Roxana, Illustration 105
Walton, Brenda, Calligraphy and Illustration 12
Weisz Yang Dunkelberger, Inc. 40
Weller Institute for the Cure of Design 41, 54, 55
Williams, Lowell, Design 150
Wilson Creative Services 76
Wolk, Michael, Design 24
Yelaska, Bruce, Design 96
Yelton/Kennerly, Inc. 158
Zemke, Deborah, Illustration 8
Zimble, Sondra, Design 34

ART DIRECTORS/DESIGNERS

Anderson, Charles Spencer 48, 132, 146
Anderson, Jack 128
Appleton, Robert 39, 156
Barnhart, Teddie 14
Batko, Chuck 166
Berry, Janae 160
Biro, Robert 47
Blik, Tyler 28
Boehm, Janis 136
Braun, Gaylen 66
Brock, Michael 66
Buck, Gary C. 50
Burns, Gael 163
Carr, Greg 152
Chamberlain, Mark 101
Collins, Brian 38
Connelly, Rosemary 64
Conte, Christina 32
Cook, Roger 60
Cooper, JoAnne 30
Covey, Traci O'Very 116
Crolick, Sue 72, 113, 168
Curtis, Laurie 112
D'Agostino, Anthony 107
Darnell, Tom 37
Davis, Nancy 86
DeFino, Perri 90
Duda, Tony 68
Dunkelberger, David 40
Dunlavey, Lindy 20, 22, 63
Dunlavey, Michael 6, 20, 22, 63
Dunnahoe, Hugh 118
Dyer, Rod 103
Eberhardt, Carol 157
Eberle, Linda 138
Emery, John 130
Feinstein, Barry 56
Fisher, Jill 80
Flanagan, Robert 114
Fox, Brian D. 47
Frankle, Rob 60
Friedman, Julius 157
Gagnon, W. Joseph 81
Gardner, Bill 26
Georgiann, Margaret 7
Gibbons, Tracy 136
Gladych, Marianne 74
Gobel, Doug 70
Grigg, Steven 11
Grimes, Melissa 110
Grossman, Myron 16
Hafeman, William 124
Hagen, Paul 166

Harrell, David **148**
Hartford, Tim **151**
Heimann, Jim **114**
Hiller, Jim **100**
Homan, William **71**
Hornall, John **143**
Hubbard, Ann Morton **25**
Hughes, Nancy Neal **148**
Jacomini, Ronald **68**
Kennedy, Michael **93, 115**
Kent, Lisa Million **104**
Kilmer, Kira **58**
Krommes, Beth **139**
Lang, Donna **123**
LaPine, Julia **116, 142**
Lawlor, Tracy **36**
Leather, Mary **173**
Lesh, David **46**
Lesniewicz, Terry **134**
Licher, Bruce **36**
Lieser, Ron **92**
Liew, Dan **98**
Linschoten, Bud **52**
Lopez-Bonilla, Juan **78**
Luck, Cindy **84**
Lyles, Lizabeth Kelly **17**
Mantels-Seeker, Ed **37**
Mayeda, Scott **102**
McGeoch, Mark **164**
Meister, Michael **36**
Minnick, Norm **108**
Mires, Scott **82**
Moberly, Laura **170**
Moeller, Karen **88**
Montezon, Greg **164**
Morales, Raymond **172**
Morla, Jennifer **173**
Napoles, Veronica **33**
Newbold, Dave **11**
Nuijens, Tom **18, 95**
Obata, Kiku **37**
Passehl, Christopher **156**
Phillips, Jennifer **155**
Phillips, Michael V. **106**
Pierantozzi, Sandi **162**
Pirtle, Woody **141**
Profancik, Larry A. **78**
Rauchman, Bob **126, 153**
Richardson, Forrest **64**
Richardson, Valerie **64**

Rubin, Bruce **71**
Salisbury, Michael **84**
Schifanella, Tom **94, 95**
Schulte, Lynn **115**
Seifer, Barry **88**
Selak, James L. **144**
Shalit, Eric **61**
Shanosky, Don **60**
Shea, Cheryl Lilley **127**
Shen, Juliet **143**
Shepherd, Robin **18**
Sickle, Ellen J. **46**
Skolos, Nancy **29, 59**
Slothower, Andrew **44**
Smentowski, Sharon **88**
Smith, Lauren **22, 123**
Sommese, Lanny **77**
Spitzley, Gale **28**
Stern, Susan **158**
Sturdivant, Ray **23**
Suchanec, Matthew **42**
Supplee, Bonnie **170**
Swormstedt, Dwayne **130**
Taflan, Peter **62**
Tanagi, Julie **143**
Th'ng, Charlie **140**
Tonn, Peter **10**
Trapp, Tom **100**
Trossman, Michael **120**
Vernon, Mindy **126, 153**
Villa, Roxana **105**
Walter, Bob **154**
Walton, Brenda **12**
Wedeen, Steve **101**
Weinberg, Allen **86**
Weller, Don **41, 54, 55**
Werner, Sharon **48**
White, Charlotte **62**
Williams, Lowell **150**
Wilson, Daniel C. **76**
Wolk, Michael **24**
Yee, Kevin **6**
Yelaska, Bruce **96**
Yelton, Jeffrey **158**
Zekanis, Lenore **42**
Zemke, Deborah **8**
Zimble, Sondra **34**

ILLUSTRATORS PHOTOGRAPHERS CALLIGRAPHERS TYPOGRAPHERS

Anderson, Charles Spencer **48, 132**
Barnhart, Teddie **14**
Boldt, Tanya **32**
Buck, Gary C. **50**
Bulgrin, Gerry **18**
Burns, Gael **163**
Carr, E.J. **120**
Chamberlain, Mark **101**
CityType **96**
Cober, Alan E. **46**
Cooper, JoAnne **30**
Curtis, Laurie **112**
D'Agostino, Anthony **107**
Darnell, Tom **37**
Davis, Nancy **86**
Dean, Bruce **160**
Derhacopian, Ron **47**
DigiType **64**
Dolginoff, Lisa **150**
Duda, Tony **68**
Dunnahoe, Hugh **118**
Fields, Dave **78**
Findlay, Stuart **94**
Fisher, Jill **80**
Flanagan, Robert **114**
Georgiann, Margaret **7**
Giannetti, Joe **72**
Gladych, Marianne **74**
Gobel, Doug **70**
Grabow, Mark **143**
Great Faces **72, 113, 168**
Grimes, Melissa **110**
Grossman, Myron **116**
Hartford, Tim **151**
Hillside Setting **33**
Hunt Type **160**
Keller, Tom **66**
Kent, Lisa Million **104**
Krogstad, Greg **128**
Krommes, Beth **139**
La Favor, Mark **168**
LaPine, Julia **142**
Leather, Mary **173**
Lithographics **8**

Lyles, Lizabeth Kelly **17**
Lynch, Warren **108**
Mantels-Seeker, Ed **37**
Marchese, Frank **156**
Morales, Raymond **172**
Naranjo, Julian **76**
New England Typographic Service **156**
Ogai, Masaaki **98**
P&H Photo Composition **71**
Phillips, Jennifer **155**
Phillips, Michael V. **106**
Pirtle, Woody **141**
Prejean, Becky O'Bryan **170**
Rager, Christi **124**
Roberts, Scott **58**
Schifanella, Tom **95**
Schulte, Lynne **48, 115**
Severson, Kent **113**
Shalit, Eric **61**
Slothower, Andrew **44**
Smith, Lauren **122, 123**
Sommese, Lanny **77**
Stanholtzer, Pamela **94**
Stipe, Michael **36**
Sturdivant, Ray **23**
Swanson, Fred **86**
Thompson Type **28**
Total Typography **144**
Tristin, Inc. **60**
Tryba, Eric **124**
Tseng, Charlene **32**
Typesmiths, The **151**
Typographic House **39**
Villa, Roxana **105**
Walton, Brenda **12**
Weller, Don **41, 54, 55**
Whitaker, Rose **148**
Wilson, Daniel C. **76**
WordTech, Inc. **38**
Zemke, Deborah **8**
Zimble, Sondra **34**
Zumbo, Matt **10**